Architecture in Pi

Is It All About Image?

Published in Great Britain in 2004 by Wiley-Academy,
a division of John Wiley & Sons Ltd

Copyright © 2004 John Wiley & Sons Ltd, The Atrium,
Southern Gate, Chichester, West Sussex PO19 8SQ, England
Telephone (+44) 1243 779777

Email (for orders & customer service enquiries): cs-books@wiley.co.uk
Visit our Home Page on www.wileyeurope.com or www.wiley.com

This publication is designed to provide accurate and authoritative
information in regard to the subject matter covered. It is sold on the
understanding that the Publisher is not engaged in rendering
professional services. If professional advice or other expert assistance
is required, the services of a competent professional should be sought.

Other Wiley Editorial Offices

John Wiley & Sons Inc., 111 River Street,
Hoboken, NJ 07030, USA

Jossey-Bass, 989 Market Street,
San Francisco, CA 94103-1741, USA

Wiley-VCH Verlag GmbH, Boschstr. 12,
D-69469 Weinheim, Germany

John Wiley & Sons Australia Ltd, 33 Park Road,
Milton, Queensland 4064, Australia

John Wiley & Sons (Asia) Pte Ltd, 2 Clementi Loop #02-01,
Jin Xing Distripark, Singapore 129809

John Wiley & Sons Canada Ltd, 22 Worcester Road,
Etobicoke, Ontario, Canada M9W 1L1

ISBN 047086690X

Cover and book design:
Christian Küsters, CHK Design, London

Printed and bound in Italy by Conti Tipocolor

Architecture in Practice

Is It All About Image?

Laura Iloniemi

CONTENTS

Foreword

Edwin Heathcote
Financial Times Architecture Critic

Architects are like novelists. They regard the most important thing in their careers as being published. Buildings are all very well but they are somehow only truly complete when they have appeared in a glossy mag. This conception of the printed page as the final fix, as part of the finishing process, has given birth to an architectural culture obsessed with publicity, in which magazines jostle for exclusives from the most fashionable practices. Yet it is an extraordinarily incestuous culture: architectural magazines are read almost entirely by other architects who do not commission buildings and are, in fact, the competition. We know that this type of publicity is important – after all, architects appear on juries, panels and advisory bodies – and this kind of prestige counts. There is a very curious condition in architecture where peer status has an excessively high value, but often at the expense of wider publicity. Architecture is alone in this approach. The weekend papers are stuffed with interviews with the same celebs pushing their latest film or book. This is not the case with buildings. Architecture does not get much press outside its own gated community, only appearing in the broadsheets (and these have actually only taken an interest in the last couple of decades).

This is what needs to change: architects must become part of the broader culture, but to do that they have to market themselves and their ideas. The loss of universal architectural grammar, of narrative, of reference and of the classical education which would have allowed cultivated viewers to read a building, has meant that architecture has to be explained. It is, unfortunately, not enough to build well, just as it is not enough to write well but appear only in tiny circulation literary journals.

Then there's buzz, the kind of cachet that goes with extreme hipness, celebrity clients and so on, but there's not much else. So how do architects publicise or market their work to the widest possible audience? Perhaps by designing exemplary buildings? Good architecture is indispensable but it is not enough on its own.

Architects from Le Corbusier to Koolhaas have found that writing books helps. A building with a manifesto is always more complete. However, you have to say something people want to hear. It doesn't, though, have to mean anything. It doesn't even have to be about your own buildings. Just think of all those seminars and discussions you've been to with fascinating themes where architects inevitably talk exclusively and excruciatingly about their latest buildings. Who wants to hear that?

Then there are monographs. Architectural publishing is increasingly becoming a vanity industry with practices paying the publisher or agreeing to buy a certain amount of books. Is there anything to put in the monograph? It doesn't matter. Think of all the books published about the best known architects and their media pull before they built anything; acres of waffle all add to the aura of mystery. And there you have the final problem: how to appear aloof and exclusive whilst getting as much published as possible? It is a curious – and very hard to pin down – blend of flannel and prescience. Within all the waffle, there has to be a few nuggets, something quotable which, while it may not actually say anything, will excite interest or propose something radical.

This will make you famous. It may get you noticed. If it is combined with the creation of eye-catching (which doesn't necessarily mean garish) architecture, it might even get you work. The opportunity to build is what this whole charade is really about. Striving for publicity may seem anathema, it may be superficial and it is certainly expensive in terms of time and of money. However, it is rarely a waste of time in an age where the primary architectural experience for most people who will see your building comes not from a visit, but from the pages of a magazine. You can succeed without publicity. But it will be harder.

Is It All About Image?

Paranoia, Pride, Perspective, Personality, Passion, Pop

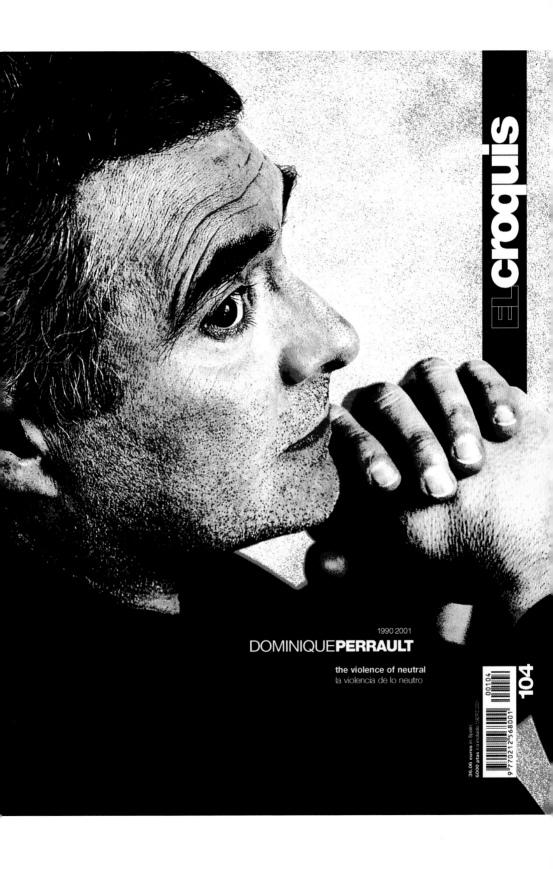

EL croquis

1990 2001

DOMINIQUE**PERRAULT**

the violence of neutral
la violencia de lo neutro

104

36.06 euros in Spain
6.000 ptas iva incluido IVPC 2001

00104

9 770212 568001

Is it all about image? In a field such as architecture one could argue, yes, of course. Images are, after all, the primary tool for developing architectural concepts, from early sketches to what have become increasingly sophisticated three-dimensional computer renderings and live footage depicting buildings. Yet, the issue of the public image of architecture appears to be, at times, a hypersensitive one. It is much easier to broach the topic of public relations and marketing in other areas of business. For instance, the manufacturers of cars, furniture and other design related products, not to mention conglomerates that mass-produce everyday consumer goods, all see self-promotional activity as a very acceptable and necessary part of their communications and sales policies.

In fields like architecture, the notion of self-promotion is met with a far more complex set of inhibitions and concerns. These arise from real doubts about whether the profession should be seen to be pushing its wares to the potential client. Should not art speak for itself, or at least be critically acclaimed by attracting awards and praise from experts reviewing the latest buildings?

Is there not something inherently distasteful about being seen to be vying for the eye of the media, clamouring for attention and recognition? Alternatively, could this just be about good business sense, an effort to secure more work and, more specifically, attracting the types of clients one would value.

As a general rule, one could say that the more commercial the practice, the more objective and business-minded the architects working there are about public relations. In contrast, the more a practice, such as a design studio, associates itself with the art world and is removed from corporate life, the more an architect's approach to public relations becomes distant from its business plan. Somewhere between the worlds of the highly commercial practices and the high-end design studios, there is a middle ground that sets the scene for how architects can benefit from public relations in a way that is most effective. It is about communicating to both client and peer group in a manner that is specifically tailored for this purpose. The printed media is the most familiar and receptive forum for this communication to take place and, above all, it is found in the pages of professional architectural publications, which are also referred to as the trade press.

Getting one's name into the trade publications is not as futile a task as many may think. Practices, more often than not, do not value the

Page 9

El Croquis **cover**

The Spanish publication *El Croquis* is one of the best-presented architectural magazines in the world. As a result, being published by *El Croquis* is a sought after honour for architects even though the profile it achieves is very much of a strictly professional nature.

The covers of the magazine feature portraits of architects, such as this one of Dominique Perrault, thus playing on the cult of the creator, not unlike *Blueprint* used to do in the 1980s

This page and overleaf

Wilkinson Eyre, Magna, Rotherham, 2001

Wilkinson Eyre invested in excellent visuals by Melon Studio of the Magna Science Adventure Centre which were coveted by the architectural press early on. This created a positive image of the project prior to its completion and most certainly paved the way for it winning the prestigious RIBA Jim Stirling Prize for Architecture in 2001.

This is a strong example of a reputation made through the recognition of one's peers

influence that the high esteem of their colleagues and the architectural circles in general can have in securing work. This influence is a result of procurement methods which rely heavily on recommendations, juries and independent architectural advisers, many of whom will source their view from the pages of trade publications and the like. In this way, architecture is a distinct field and unusually self-sufficient in making reputations, unlike, for instance, the music or fashion industries that rely heavily on popular ratings and street credibility. No wonder architects are notorious for not being as good as so many other representatives of the creative industries in their attempt to get their message out.

Anyone who has tried their hand at publicity will know that it is hard work. While one may despair about how to get a grip on managing the various PR activities in an office, from labelling images to sending out press notices, one may also reconsider how effective PR is as a means of communication with respect to what one really wants to say. One of the reasons architects shy away from PR is that, unlike academic discourse, promotional language is expected to be shallow or too flowery. It is true that in the field of public relations too many consultants think that merely singing the praises of a project will grab the attention of the media and general public alike.

This book is written on the premise that, because architecture as a industry tends to attract well-educated critics, writers, broadcasters and presenters, as well as clients, the rule of thumb should be to express knowledge and intelligence. Press releases should be upbeat, of course, but usually what is appreciated most is good, accurate, well-researched and well-presented information. The case for why something is good should not be based on opinion as much as a well-argued analysis of the situation or the facts that support one's cause. Generic blurb should be avoided as the architectural circles' communication levels tend to be above the usual bland corporate speak. Too often, one's eyes glaze over at the same words, so similar that only the name of the practice seems to have been changed, with the rest of the copy remaining virtually the same.

If PRs fall into the trap of describing all the latest projects in too slogan-like or adjectival terms, then architects fall into a trap of thinking that they could up their media presence in a similar way to pop stars. It has become popular for practices to use hip, rock band-like names in an effort to dissociate themselves from 'boring architects'. Brochure covers are designed to look like album covers and overall graphics are reminiscent

Future Systems, Selfridges, Birmingham, 2003

One of the best covered buildings in Britain in 2003, the Selfridges Birmingham store has captured the public's imagination partly because it is intended as a landmark and is accessible to all, and partly because it houses a popular activity, shopping. It is futuristic and perceivable as innovative fun, not unlike like a James Bond movie set. The selection of Future Systems as architects for the project works well in furthering the brand value of Selfridges and creating a 'destination of the moment'. In this way, the architects have created positive PR and image value for their client

This page and overleaf
Toyo Ito with Arup, Serpentine
Gallery Summer Pavilion,
London, 2002
Recurring architectural events
at venues that attract
audiences with a general
interest in the arts are ideal
ways of promoting buildings
and practitioners to the
public. The Serpentine Gallery
Summer Pavilions have been
effective in making this sort
of impact and allowing visitors
to experience in full how
works by some of the world's
leading architects actually feel
as spaces

Is It All About Image?

of the world of consumer goods advertising, with a tongue-in-cheek, lightweight irony that is more in tune with ad agency jingles than the heavy business of building. As a phenomenon this may seem to be innocuous, but it has led to confusion about how practices should promote themselves.

The debate about whether it is acceptable to 'push' art has led many designers to imitate the music industry in a manner that is generally, if not accurately, considered to be credible rather than commercial. Yet, as not one architect has reached anything close to the cult status of so many popular performing artists, writers and painters, one is forced to ask whether the public imaging methods of other creative industries can be sucessfully applied to architecture.

The overall complexity of how architects can stand out from their peers lies within the general lack of public perception of the built environment. It is very difficult to craft a niche or have a voluble message within a

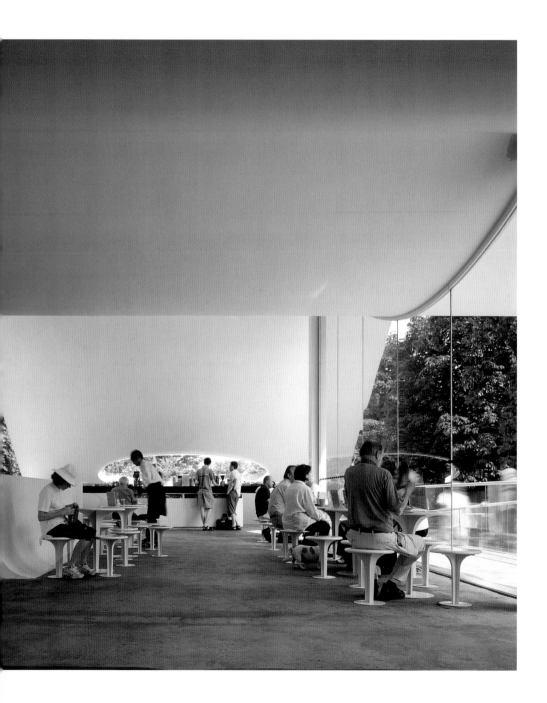

Is It All About Image?

profession that, as a whole, is badly promoted. To have a voice that is distinct amongst musicians is not difficult as the general public knows enough about the music scene to distinguish recent and contemporary movements such as rave, dance music and metal and to determine who the cult figures are in each one. Such familiarity does not exist with buildings, even though they literally surround our every day lives.
In other words, the general public does not tend to know enough about the architecture scene to formulate an opinion as to what one aspect of it may mean in relation to another. Modernism and minimalism are often considered synonymous. It is thus very demanding for a practice to position its architectural philosophy within this current climate.

This said, architects should not feel that it is their mission as individual practitioners to raise the profile of an entire profession. A practice cannot hope to single-handedly lift the state of architecture by taking on educational or curatorial projects that do not directly relate to the practice's own marketing goals. Such work should be left to the institutions whose sole mission is to activate public awareness of architecture. There is no reason that individual architects cannot support such organisations whilst raising their own stakes in the design community as the opinion leaders, public figures and movers and shakers whom the media seek out for comment.

A book on PR and architecture would be expected to advocate that, in general, PR is a worthwhile pursuit for architects. However, throughout the book the question of how a PR strategy for an architectural practice should be crafted is kept as open as possible. The book is intended to be a guide that gives the reader the scope to see what is being done out there, what works for some and perhaps not for others. A diversity

Below

***Blueprint* cover**

Blueprint evoked the cult of the creator in the 1980s, featuring Eva Jiricna on its first cover. As one of *Blueprint*'s founders, Peter Murray remarks on publishing versus promotion, 'Publishing was not about promoting architecture but defining process, what it is about. Now physical aspects of buildings and fashionableness or image, not process and social benefits are the focus ... I feel a bit guilty for this as *Blueprint* was more responsible than any other organ for promoting architects as stars ... We put portraits on the cover because I had found out that sales of *Vogue* went up by 20 percent when the cover figure made eye contact with the purchaser.'

London's magazine of design, architecture and style/Number one/October 1983/Price 95p

STYLE: EVA JIRICNA'S SHOPS BRITISH ARCHITECTURE NOW
SEBASTIAN CONRAN'S FIRST BUS MILAN'S BEST PARTIES
PETER YORK ON THE MEANING OF CLOTHES

Is It All About Image?

of approaches has been included here so that the reader, should they be an architect, may determine what might best suit their practice.

It is recognised throughout the book that practitioners vary not only with respect to the size of their operation, and thus their human resources, but also in what drives them. What might be considered a hugely embarrassing self-promotional activity in one practice may be just the thing for another in its attempts to make friends or influence people in a beneficial manner.

Finally, to return to our question briefly: is it all about image? Well, the tools of publicity are heavily image oriented, as are its products: press and live coverage. Even lectures are visual while, as for radio, slots are limited when it comes to the built environment. In concrete terms, image is thus king. In more abstract terms, image need not only be what lies on the surface. One can certainly penetrate beyond the surface and truly push ideas as a part of one's media campaign. If one has a strong design concept, it needs to be articulated in a manner that speaks to the media.

Far too frequently, architects are misled into thinking that a milestone for their practice will be of interest outside their peer group. The good old cocktail party trick is not a bad one – 'Am I boring everyone around me by talking about this? Can I express it in a way that makes my latest achievement relevant to those around me?' Much of PR is about just that: relating to the public. If one has nothing to say or doesn't know how to say it, the launch parties and freebie lunches will not mask an inability to get something pertinent or engaging across.

Praxis: Where do PRs fit in?

Much has been made of the increasing popularity of design in the past decade or so. In the United Kingdom, the national media has its architectural correspondents and design or interiors editors, while around the world there is an ever increasing plethora of lifestyle magazines that feature modern homes, interiors in general and, more recently, the latest in groovy restaurant, hotel and occasionally even office design. Practices have been quick to pick up on such exposure as ideal for acquiring new clients or persuading existing clients of the merits of their work.

The design press tends to be good at transforming the sometimes dry project information received from practices into whatever is more suitable for their readers to digest on the pages of glossies, supplements or newsprint. Pitching a not obviously glamorous story to non-design specialist writers in the consumer media can, of course, be a bit trickier and this is when the services of a public relations consultant are certainly appreciated.

Of course, PRs should not be seen only as those who promote stories that are difficult to place in the media. Architects, and others experienced in media relations, will know that PRs can be equally valuable in placing "easy" high-profile stories by virtue of maximising or directing coverage in a way that is most beneficial to their client.

For example, a PR campaign can be organised to both play down and highlight aspects of a project. An architect may want to dissociate the practice from the chintzy interior designs that a consultant was brought in to do as a part of a project or, conversely, associate the practice with a particularly successful exhibition. Sometimes it is very telling to consider the jobs that some practices choose not to publish at all, such as house extensions or commercial bread and butter work. In other words, architects can use PR as a means to control how their work is seen in respect to the practice's areas of interest. This is a very strategic way to use PR in terms of long term views on influencing the types of projects a practice would like to attract.

At the end of a job, when feelings between the architects and their client can be running riot as the last stages of a building are nearing completion, it is also often handy to bring in a neutral person on the PR front. Too often, opportunities for good media exposure are missed because the architect in question does not think it appropriate to bring up the vain topic of PR. There is also a fear of the architect's client thinking, 'What an egomaniac who cares less about my building than about

The Arup Asociates Brochure
In its 40th year, London-based
Arup Associates produced a
practice brochure in-house.
Designed by Nik Browning,
the document reflects the
ethos of the practice with its
interest in multidisciplinary
design, innovation, continuity
and sustainability. It is very
much a design that is
identifiable with the face
of the practice, no doubt a
benefit of having been
produced by the practice's
own graphics department

The Arup Associates Graphics
To celebrate four decades
of practice, Arup Associates
organised a lecture series
at the Royal Society of Arts
in London. The idea was to
reflect on issues important
to the practice's work without
having a monographic
approach. Led by Nik
Browning, the Arup Associates
Graphics Team produced
a consistent set of graphics
from letterheads to lecture
tickets and press releases
for the event

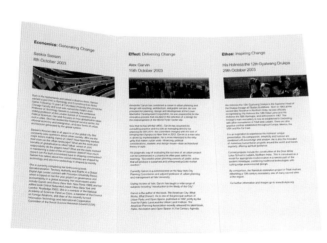

**Left and below
Featherstone Associates,
Logo and Shakers**
Sarah Featherstone of
Featherstone Associates
in London has long been
interested in how architects
communicate their work.
She has explored how to
make her practice's work
more accessible via exhibitions
and public consultation
exercises. The logo used by
Featherstone – the crest –
is indicative of the truly
service oriented and even
boutique-like quality of the
practice. Featherstone has
also used playful items,
such as snow shakers
with miniature models of
buildings inside, designed
by the practice in an effort
to get people to think about
architecture afresh

Is It All About Image?

Below
The Broadway Malyan
Brochure
Photec designed a small
booklet for architects
Broadway Malyan. The
document is ideas- rather than
building-focused, quoting from
the Modernist heroes like
Mies and using photography
in a reportage-like fashion.
Overall, the effect is not
dissimilar to that found in
the world of advertising.
It is very much about drawing
the recipient's attention, not
to the buildings (the product)
designed by the practice, but
to the image that Broadway
Malyan wishes to create or
convey

Right
Fluid postcard
As the name suggests, Fluid is
a practice that seeks to look at
design in as broad a way as
possible. The London-based
architects have created a set of
postcards that describe their
areas of work: consultation;
masterplanning; architecture;
communication. As the card on
consultation suggests, the
approach is very much about
workshops, public open days
and other ways of gauging
public opinion. The message:
Fluid's work is a response
generated by understanding
the needs of the future
occupants and users of built
environments

commissioning photographs and getting promotional value out of the
project in order to move on before the builders have even left my site'.

Throughout the life span of a project, PRS come in handy with their
ability to reassure the architects' clients that issues such as confidentiality,
exclusivity to certain publications and overall media management are
handled more professionally. This, in return, tends to assist the architect
as it allows for more goodwill from the project client towards the
publicising of a design.

Beyond a media liaison role, there can be a more marketing-oriented
role for the person charged with PR in a practice, be it someone in-house
or a consultant who has been brought in especially for this purpose. PRS
can be very useful in thinking up how best to interface with clients who
may not be that design savvy. After all, the non-designer is a good judge
of what can be assimilated or appealing to the layperson.

The same information and presentation materials do not necessarily
adequately respond to the needs of both clients and media. Many

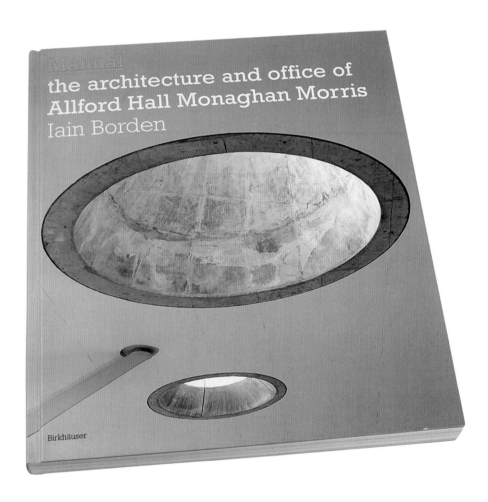

the architecture and office of
Allford Hall Monaghan Morris
Iain Borden

Manual

Birkhäuser

Opposite and below
Manual: The Architecture and Office of Allford Hall Monaghan Morris published by Birkhäuser Verlag AG, written by the Bartlett School of Architecture Director Iain Borden

Practice monographs have been the book de rigueur as of recent years. Quite a few architects have realised that they need not be much more expensive to produce than full fledged glossy brochures and, if done properly by a reputable publisher, are much better advocates for one's work: third party accreditation. You will increasingly find that a large number of medium sized and relatively young practices have books written by academics and the like on their work. Allford Hall Monagham Morris's practice brochure called the *Manual* has opted for the thematic route to convey a message beyond that of the traditional practice monograph. This is clever in that the book avoids the boredom of a catalogue of projects found in many such publications. The lay-out of the *Manual* too avoids the repetition typical of project data sheet formats that fill most architects' brochures making these rather relentless to peruse.

S, M, L, XL, **written by Rem Koolhaas, designed by Bruce Mau and published in 1995 by 010 of Rotterdam**
The architectural contingent is so formulaic in its modes of presentation that *S, M, L, XL*, by virtue of looking different – a weighty tome with the page size of a novel – immediately became iconic and much mimicked. Such ploys would certainly have not been as remarkable amongst other creative industries. Yes, architecture is still very much a profession that needs occasional mavericks like Rem to rev things up

Is It All About Image?

practices have benefited, for example, from two sets of photography on projects: one that shows how the buildings can be used by its occupants, which is naturally of interest to potential clients, and another set which focuses more on the compositional, sculptural and other potentially poetic qualities of a project that would enthuse the architectural critic.

In the same vein, practices that communicate well with their clients tend to write up thematic texts on their buildings which explain their design ethos, or how a building benefits its environment, without using the kind of jargon and technical detail that they would include in a project description for the specialist press.

This type of targeting adds up to a lot of work. There is no doubt that the promotion of a practice is not a small task. The brutal reality is that in order to do it properly, more often than not, one is almost doubling up on written and visual materials.

These days, architects are also doing more and more on the PR front. Desktop publishing has made it possible for a one-man-band to have a full colour brochure. Perhaps, as a result, more established practices have decided they need a properly published book to enhance their standing in the profession. Even very young practices, with only a handful of completed works, are getting monographs published. What better calling card for the less experienced practitioner than a third party accreditation – a publisher – saying that this designer is worthy of a book? Yet all this means that to remain competitive, one always needs to keep up-to-date on the image front.

In addition to the printed media, architects' practices, like most other businesses, are creating a presence for themselves on the internet which requires specialist skills in their offices either to design or update websites. Even responding to media queries properly requires someone who keeps track of images and copyright issues. Just managing a digital library to produce all these marketing or PR tools is time consuming. One might just give up now and say, 'I don't want to know what else I should be doing, or doing better, as I don't have the resources to set up a PR department'. Perhaps, before coming to this conclusion, it is worth seeing in the following chapters how a number of practices from different countries cope by resorting to all sorts of different combinations of resources and methods for dealing with their promotional needs.

PR ladies
Pegs
Push
Promotion
Prudence
Parlance

The publicist case studies look at the variation in using in-house publicists, as do London-based firms Arup and Foster and Partners, and out-of-house specialist consultants like Cohn Davis Bigar in New York. Some practices, such as Will Alsop in London, combine these approaches and some manage things between their partners, as does New York-based SHoP. Helsinki design studio Ocean North is a good example of how a virtually one-man-band can be successful in PR terms.

The different ways publicists and architects view PR are very telling. Publicists know the game and realise that to win you need to play it by the rules of the media: use soundbites, keep pitches punchy and aim for topicality. Architects tend to want to document their stories for the public in too much detail – beyond what is relevant for the purposes of the media. Often, architects fret too much about the occasional imprecision about their practice or work. At the same time, they often deny that they are interested in publicity. For example, a few highly media-savvy practices did not want to be interviewed for a book such as this one that might reveal the fact that they do seek publicity.

Harriett Hindmarsh, Arup, London

Laura Iloniemi

It would be not an exaggeration to say that Arup is the world's leading engineering firm. The practice is working on prestigious projects internationally, such as the new World Trade Center buildings in New York with Studio Libeskind, the 2008 Beijing Olympic Stadium with Herzog & de Meuron and Swiss Re Headquarters (called 'The Gherkin') in London with Foster and Partners. Arup is constantly sought after for collaboration on design teams by architects of the calibre of those just mentioned. Yet, one of the main difficulties for Arup, in PR terms, is to get recognition for its role even on major projects.

If architects find it a challenge to make headlines, by comparison the situation is an even trickier one for engineers. Harriett Hindmarsh, media relations manager at Arup, says that, 'The profile of engineering is a big obstacle. Journalists love architects because they are the artist, personality, ego. The people who wear funky glasses and clothes … Engineering is integral to building, it is part of the design but that just does not seem interesting.'

To tackle this lack of innate appetite amongst the media for engineering stories, Hindmarsh has opted for a proactive approach for Arup's PR Department. The department's title emphasises a distinction from a press office that is primarily reactive and can even be dealing with a larger than desired influx of media queries. As Hindmarsh says, '60% of what we do is finding stories to package and sell … We have to be a lot more proactive than other types of design firms.'

The need to be proactive applies for most architectural practices. Few have stories like the opening of Bilbao Guggenheim which the media are hungry to cover. The example of Arup is also a critical one because it highlights the issue of not only getting

coverage on a project, but making sure that one is credited. How many people know the names of the designers, never mind the engineers, behind even the best publicised projects like the London Eye?

To get recognition for what Arup does, Hindmarsh has found it essential to work with the PR departments of those who commission the buildings: Arup's clients. She says, 'Unless you are with your client, you have no chance. It helps to work as part of a team, each telling different aspects of a story'. It is certainly true that the types of commissioning bodies that are funding the construction of a new building tend to prefer that the publicity of the projects is dealt with in a professional and well-orchestrated manner. If not, they prefer to leave the designers out of the limelight. If so, they may even welcome some extra coverage in the press that they would not otherwise have thought of, or have access to, in their pursuit of PR mileage.

In addition to Harriett Hindmarsh and the press officer who assists her, Arup employs a head of corporate communications, a team of six graphic designers, a publications team of two who produce the *Arup Journal* and internal publications as well as a website team of four. There is a real investment in getting the global message right both to the members of staff in over a hundred countries and to the outside world. The practice has also realised that, as a part of a successful marketing strategy, it pays to make what it does as a business better understood.

Engineering can be a daunting subject even for a clever layperson and Hindmarsh describes much of what she does as 'decoding' or 'creating a bridge between engineers, the work we do and the rest of the world which makes it easier for everyone else'.

**Harriett Hindmarsh, Media
Relations Manager at work**
Hindmarsh has gained a
reputation amongst the media
for being straightforward and
informative, yet proud of the
integrity and skills of the
engineers she represents. What
better ambassador for Arup

Below
SPEAR **Postcard**
As an accessible (and, to boot,
media friendly) way to measure
and visualise sustainability
credentials, Arup created
SPEAR. Harriett Hindmarsh
hosted a launch to present and
demonstrate this reporting tool.
This exemplifies an effective
way to take credit for Arup's
invention and inform interested
parties

Above
**World Architecture Awards
Ceremony**
Arup has sponsored the World
Architecture Awards two years
in a row as it provides good
exposure amongst architects
who are a key source to
commissioning the engineers.
Moreover, the Awards promote
the design team as a whole,
including consultants,
which is in keeping with
Arup's belief in an integrated
approach to design

A PR's advantage to the expert can be just this:
an ability to better understand what is being asked
and perhaps not strictly from a technical point of
view. A good PR can relay this to the expert in a
way that does not make them feel their work is
being misunderstood, oversimplified or undervalued.
It is in this way that the PR becomes an ally to
their clients who might otherwise think that publicity
compromises what they do and, at the same time,
feel the frustration of not getting the acknowledgement
they believe they deserve for their work. As
Hindmarsh explains, 'PR is against what engineers
are used to. They know their services are valuable.
To have to prove that to a magazine is hard.'

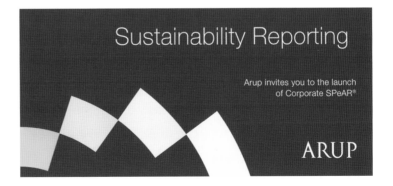

Left
Arup Associates and Arup,
The Druk White Lotus
School, Ladakh, Northern
India, 2001–
Arup, together with Arup
Associates, which includes
architects, has designed the
Druk White Lotus School
in Ladakh, Northern India.
The design work is done *pro
bono* and is a good example
of goodwill PR whilst investing
in developing sustainable
architecture and modernising
the world in a way that
represents the designers'
ethos. The project has won
numerous accolades and
generated media interest in a
topic that is perhaps not
fashionable but all the more
significant in terms of how
developing countries secure
their future identity and
environment

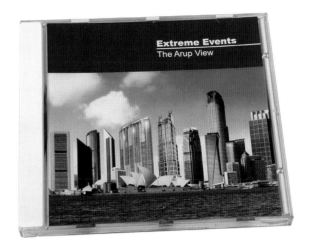

Extreme Events
The Arup View

" A design team which produces a total, balanced, efficient design can help to produce a better environment. "

Sir Ove Arup, November 1968

Opposite
World Trade Center
After the events of 11 September 2001, Arup prepared a report called *Extreme Events* to help clients and the construction industry to understand the events from a structural perspective. Part of the mission was to improve the design of high-rise buildings but also to be a reference point for media and other queries. It would be cynical to say that this was a PR ploy because the report does represent the very core of the Arup Group's values about learning, sharing and disseminating information internationally. Fortunately, Arup had the PR resources to get this valuable information across to as wide an audience as possible

Below
World Architecture
Award Postcard
To let their clients and media know why Arup are behind the World Architecture Awards, Hindmarsh set up a postcard campaign with a statement from the founder of the Group, Ove Arup. The decision to show the back of his head is an ideal expression of Arup's desire to promote not individuals but the group as a whole

Katy Harris, Foster and Partners, London

Laura Iloniemi

Much has been made about how Foster and Partners is the exemplary practice in terms of handling its PR. Practices widely admire the consistency of the presentation of the work, be it in the quality of images that are published or the graphics that support information. Everything seems to be carefully thought out and controlled within an aesthetic that supports the Foster design ethos of making his buildings a little like machines. There is a delight in an industrial sensibility, in exposing the building technology and experimenting with construction in non-traditional materials such as those used for aircraft manufacturing.

The cool Foster grey and the Otl Aicher designed Rotis font (that is visually similar to Akzidenz Grotesk, 1895), have been carefully selected to convey what could be described as the Foster corporate identity. A similar graphic rigour applies to most of the Foster publications with their underlying grids and pared down visual presentation, not dissimilar to the early modernist books on architecture.

The formula works. From Foster and Partners you will receive a professionally assembled document that coveys how similar care and consideration go into everything it does, not just the buildings but right down to the laying out of a cover letter. Some would describe this as being slick, others would say it is just about doing things properly. What comes across, though, is a practice that really is about design. There is such a passion about design that it informs everything that is done. The selecting of a font that becomes the practice's graphic identity is less a cynical branding exercise and more a heartfelt statement of the architects' vision. This is the best way for a practice to say to the world what it is

about. Too many practices now radically change their identity to suit the times or copy another practice's identity. The former's fickleness suggests a lack of conviction and the latter a lack of originality.

There is no doubt that Foster and Partners is one of the most impressive practices in terms of how well its information is organised and potentially available to the press. There is a real desire to record the work thoroughly. This is as much about being together as about taking a pleasure and pride in what you do. Katy Harris, who heads the Communications Department at Foster and Partners and has been with the practice for 22 years, started off by transferring slides into a museum-like library with sliding back-lit screens for easy viewing that Norman Foster had acquired from Germany. As a result, she got to know the work inside out and quickly became THE person who knew which were the favourite images and so forth. Harris joined Foster Associates at the time the practice won the Hongkong Shanghai Bank project. She says, 'It was the first time that press relations had been taken seriously. There was not a very coordinated approach to the issue of publicity materials'.

Birkin Haward, who joined Fosters in 1969 and later became a Director, had until Harris's time led the publicity side of things. He had been instrumental in developing the drawing style that has since been established at the practice. Haward's drawings were excellent in communicating in a fresh and accessible way what the buildings were about and how the services operated. This was helpful in pushing ideas on building efficiency and the environmental agenda to clients. Harris also says that, 'Birkin's style of drawing captured a feeling or atmosphere of a design without giving too much information about a building'.

The move to the new offices at Great Portland Street instigated a desire to get things right in terms of how visuals were organised. Like Norman Foster, Birkin Haward is a keen photographer and visibly enjoys all the apparatus. Together with Harris, Haward decided to go through all the projects and select the 'top shots' for each. This routine of vetting the favourite images to be used in pitching for jobs or for publication is still in place. Images aside, there is also a certain way that projects are written about at the practice. Rather than a florid, self-appraising style, it is instead very much an informative and academic one.

It could appear as though the desire to control the outside perception of Foster and Partners by rigorously selecting what is released into the public realm is about manipulating the media, spinning a story. Yet, looking at Foster and Partners' PR tools, it does seem like the publicity materials are there to ensure the best impression, but only in so far as a musician may want to control the way their sound is reproduced. It is, of course, true that if one visits a building it may not be quite like it appears in the press pack, and in a totally different context than one may have imagined, but it is the journalist's job to find this out for themselves.

In some ways, Foster and Partners is described as a PR machine in far too casual a way. The success of the practice is not based on seeking publicity: it is founded on doing everything to a high standard, including the PR.

The sheer range of experience in building types far outweighs the efforts that have gone into proactive PR. In fact, the promotional activity at Foster and Partners is not at all disproportionate to the work that has been done. Whatever one thinks of the work, there is also no doubt that this practice has already made a contribution to recent design history as an innovative force that has captured its time.

Harris describes much of the PR at Foster and Partners as being reactive, vetting through requests for interviews, public speaking, positions on committees and the like. Naturally, demands on Norman Foster's time are very real and these days his partners (Spencer de Grey, David Nelson, Graham Phillips and, until recently, Ken Shuttleworth) have taken on more public roles. Harris says that the media have developed relationships with the partners over the years. This of course eases off the pressure from one figurehead having to tackle the public alone.

In 2003, Foster and Partners made Harris a member of its board of directors. This means that the practice values her input and how it helps reflect what the firm wants to say about itself. What can be better than to have someone at board level who understands, from years of experience, how you want to present yourself and who is able to manage this in a practice of about 600 staff. Harris now attends the directors' meetings and is thus always up to speed on new jobs coming in and the direction of the practice. This is a great asset for anyone charged with publicity as too often the rift between the communications officers of a practice and the partners is ironically so wide that 'communications' cannot do its job properly. I ask Harris whether, at the directors' meetings, she has to report on how the PR strategy responds to the overall business plan. The answer is very telling, 'The PR strategy is the business strategy, it is all a part of the same thing. The publicity is about the work, Foster's philosophy.'

Looking at the recent books on the practice, this statement certainly rings true. There is of course the pleasure in producing the object, i.e. the book, almost like buildings in miniature. Yet there are quite a few of these objects: *The Norman Foster Catalogue of Work* (2001); *Norman Foster and The British Museum* (2001); *Foster Catalogue* (2001); *Architecture is About People: Norman Foster* (2001); *On Foster … Foster On* (2000), etc. Yes, the number of books on the practice in and of itself could be viewed as an effective promotion, giving an art historical aura to the work. This may well be the intention, too, but on the other hand the books just display a desire for Norman Foster to write about his work almost as a scholarly exercise, to make sense of it and to explain it. Like many architects, he seems to think that in doing what his team does, they must be able to justify it. Harris says that Norman Foster has, 'a strong sense of social responsibility, a sense of the bigger picture and the global impact of what architects do'. Without being naïve, there is a sense of civic mission in how Foster and Partners promotes itself. By doing it so very professionally, with well-produced publicity materials that are delivered to all the right people at the right time, this practice is well ahead of the game and without any fancy tricks up its sleeve.

Below
Classic Silver Press Pack
The classic Foster and Partners press pack comes in a matt silver folder with a very fact-based project description rather than an all-singing, all-dancing press release, with drawings reduced to A4 and a few photographic prints of the building. The practice employs a full-time photographer due to the sheer quantity of work. In terms of owning the copyright for their photos, this is also useful

Bottom
Foster and Partners studios, Riverside No. Three, London, 1986–90
The practice has created an environment in its studios that would feel comfortable to the business executive who is about to commission a big project. The office, with its grand entrance, exudes both professionalism and a homely sense of well-being, with small meeting tables overlooking the Thames. Everything implies a full commitment to what is being done, with a good balance between the ability to deliver and a love of the craft

Foster and Partners architects and designers London   Riverside Three   Tel 0207 738 0455
                                               Berlin   22 Hester Road   Fax 0207 738 1107706
                                               Singapore   London SW11 4AN

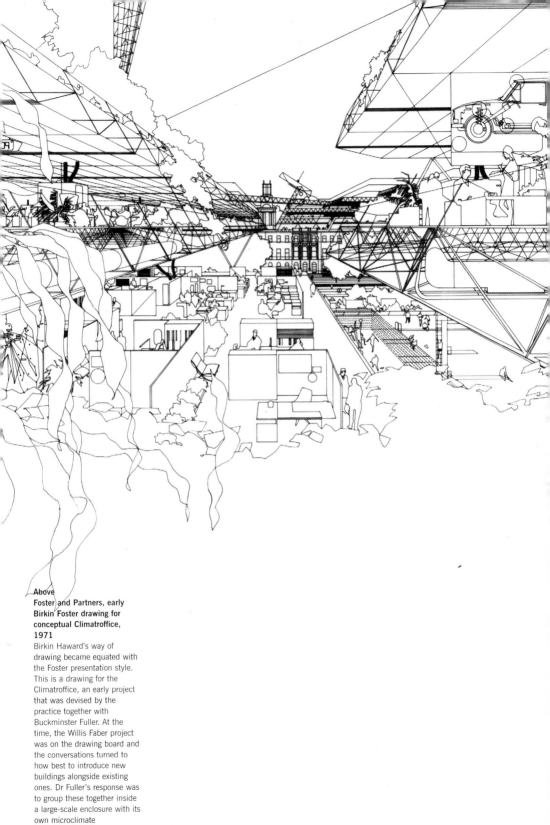

Above
Foster and Partners, early
Birkin Foster drawing for
conceptual Climatroffice,
1971
Birkin Haward's way of
drawing became equated with
the Foster presentation style.
This is a drawing for the
Climatroffice, an early project
that was devised by the
practice together with
Buckminster Fuller. At the
time, the Willis Faber project
was on the drawing board and
the conversations turned to
how best to introduce new
buildings alongside existing
ones. Dr Fuller's response was
to group these together inside
a large-scale enclosure with its
own microclimate

Left and previous spread
Foster and Partners,
30 St Mary Axe, London,
2004
Commonly referred to as
The Gherkin, 30 St Mary
Axe is perhaps currently the
best-known project by Foster
and Partners. Here the iconic
and innovative shape of the
building creates its own image.
It is such a strong one that
other new buildings
photographed against it might
increase their chances of being
published. The Millennium
Dome also once had this
cachet by underlining a
particular time in London's
building history

Bottom
Foster and Partners
Sage Gateshead, Gateshead,
2004
This Sage Gateshead project
is part of a regeneration boom
in the area attracting media
interest in the story.
As Foster and Partners write,
'Geographically, it fills the "gap
on the map" for music venues,
the nearest alternatives being
more than three hours away.
It also complements the
redevelopment of the
neighbouring Baltic Flour Mills
as a centre for contemporary
art, consolidating Tyneside's
position as an arts'
destination.' All good reasons
to write about the forthcoming
Foster project

Is It All About Image?

This page
Foster and Partners,
Sainsbury Centre for The
Visual Arts, Norwich, 1978
The Sainsbury Centre for The
Visual Arts is one of the key
buildings in the roster of work
at Foster and Partners. It is
a building used to define the
practice historically – a
highlight from the past. The
client and building type are
prestigious, which helps, but
above all the design has made
its mark in a memorable way.
The hangar-like building is
a demonstration of Norman
Foster's passion for aerospace
design which in itself is
fascinating to see applied to
architecture

Peter Carzasty/Cohn Davis Bigar Communications, New York

Laura Iloniemi

Peter Carzasty is executive vice president at New York-based Cohn Davis Bigar Communications. Until recently, he was with another leading Manhattan agency, the Kreisberg Group, which has developed a reputation for specialising in the promotion of culturally significant projects such as the revitalisation of Grand Central Station in New York and the Aga Khan Award for Architecture. The Group's high-profile client roster has included architects such as Tadao Ando, Santiago Calatrava, Eisenmann Architects, Frank O Gehry and Associates and Richard Meier and Partners.

Often, the work Kreisberg has carried out with architects has been as part of publicising a new venue or facility. Carzasty has also worked directly with global architectural names such as Calatrava who, despite having offices in Zürich, Paris and Valencia, realises the potential of having a PR presence at the heart of where his design studio's work might be most talked about. Together with London, New York is most definitely one of the epicentres of debate on new building and design.

I ask Carzasty if it is very different working for, say, an institution like a major museum than an individual architectural practice. 'An institutional profile is made up of different elements that add up to a collective awareness. For an architectural firm that bears the name of a single person there is a different agenda; you are dealing with an individual and how they are perceived. With an institution there are perhaps one or two big objectives, the brush strokes are broader. With an individual you are getting to know the personality or their own point of view, how they feel, their personal aesthetic. If you miscalculate positioning an individual and their firm

as expressed in their buildings as a part of their branding, there is less to counterbalance you than if you are dealing with an institution.' This is why Carzasty feels that in order to be an effective advocate for an architect one needs to have a very nuanced understanding of what is being said. When representing architects, this requires making an investment in getting to know each individual's way of working, their personality, professional history and ethos as well as the detail of their projects. This is just the kind of sensitivity and expertise that an architect should be buying into when considering hiring a PR consultant.

It is certainly true that promoting architecture can be a very sensitive business requiring expert skills. Emotionally charged responses are not uncommon at the end of a project that may have involved several years of difficult politics with clients, funders, planners or other bodies. Of course, such politics all too often compromise the original vision for a building. Yet, the œuvre of an architect is mostly out there to be critically appraised as a work of art, as though it was the sole result of artistic intent. The difficulty architects experience in going public with their work should be understood in this context. Moreover, as Carzasty says, 'The architect cannot come back to his work, like a choreographer, or the director of a Broadway show who can freshen up a performance by returning to the cast after a few months of a performance running'. Instead, as he points out, 'Architects really have to let go of their baby. It is the most public of artistic expressions, the most vulnerable to public display.'

This, in return, places a heightened responsibility on the nature of the PR. In architectural PR there is a

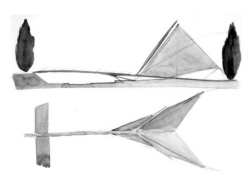

**Santiago Calatrava,
Milwaukee Art Museum,
Quadracci Pavilion,
Milwaukee, 2001**
The Milwaukee Art Museum
project is an example of where
the client has benefited from
working with an architect to
create an international and
high cultural profile for their
institution. The key for this to
take place was provided by a
combination of the architecture
itself and how it was promoted
by Kreisberg (a very subtle PR
organisation that knows art
organisations well). Milwaukee
Art Museum chose to base its
own logo on the shape of the
Calatrava building

particular tendency to need to control a campaign to
the extent of going way beyond what is necessary to
get the desired results. Sometimes this is so much so
that the perfectionism invested in getting PR materials
together compromises what is most important in a
PR campaign: the timing. No matter how good one's
publicity materials are, no matter how intelligent
the words or how well the drawings or photographs
represent the project, they are of no use once you
have missed the short life span in which the project
is still newsworthy. Perhaps, the architects who are
best at PR are able to divorce the promotion of their
work from their design work just enough to actually
let the buildings get out there for comment.

In addition to forging the PR campaign while
the iron is hot, PRs need to be able to comprehend,
predict and respond to how the media may affect the
architect as an artist. As Carzasty well understands,
'Building criticism goes to the essence of who and
what architects are. It is very internalised and
personalised. For the institutional client, the criticism
is one step removed and therefore, more often than
not, not as immediate or direct.' He adds, 'Architects
are most exposed out of the creatives. What they do
is so public and they have no final control on the
finished product. For example, public buildings and
how they are perceived depends on how they are
maintained.' Even the most perfect design can
thus be compromised and is, all said and done,
beyond the architect's control.

Sometimes, once a project is let loose for
maximum exposure, it is difficult to understand why
no-one seems interested after all the time and effort
that may have gone into completing a building and
even managing its PR properly. Some real hard truths

apply here in terms of the media interest levels for buildings. For example, Carzasty reveals from his experiences, 'There exists a pecking order in the United States according to the degrees in which the media responds. At the top are museums for the visual arts, then come dedicated concert halls and then performing arts facilities along with public cultural facilities. From public to private use the interest level decreases. For example, academic buildings are lower on the list, because they tend to be private facilities.'

It is important that, if in doubt, an architect seeks the advice of their PR in appreciating the interest level of their project. Pursuing unrealistic media targets is an unrewarding use of time, energy and money for all and can even be damaging for the architect in building up an image of a time-waster in the face of the media.

A good PR will advise their client of the PR potential for a project. As Carzasty elaborates, 'As a client is looking at you, you are also looking at the client. There needs to be communication, a shared dialogue for realistic media expectations. There are cases where I have realised client expectations are unrealistic. In these situations, you can suggest what can be done but if the client is not open to reassessing their expectations, there is no mutual benefit in carrying on because your client's perception will be that you cannot deliver.' Very appropriately, Carzasty adds, 'Your own credibility is at stake, too. I do not take on an undoable project. We want success, too.'

Anyone engaging in PR should remember that most publicists would agree that they have two clients: the media and their client. This may seem compromising to the person hiring the PR but Carzasty sheds light on the issue, 'I work 51 percent in favour of the media because they are the individuals I go back to on a regular basis. My service, my credibility is with the media ... If a specific client given goal is inappropriate to pursue with the media, I will say no to this request but pursue other avenues to see what can be done. I will not wear out my welcome with my media contacts along the way because, as I explain to our clients, "just as you have benefited from previous history of goodwill, so will others too".' What Carzasty says here really lies at the very core of good media relations management. Architects dealing with the press directly should also bear this long-term goodwill in mind.

The above implicitly tells us that good PR is not just about having a PR guru who works with what one particular client has to offer, turning their wares and abilities into media magic. It is usually more about that client benefiting from all the good work the PR had done in their years of experience with other clients, projects or social dealings with the media. It is also about sheer knowledge of the area that the PR company is working in. Without this, a publicity campaign is sure to miss many opportunities for

Left
Zoomorphic **Exhibition Invitation for the Victoria & Albert Museum**
Based on an architectural blueprint, Johnson Bank's design of the invitation was well-received

Below
Zoomorphic **Book Cover**
Santiago Calatrava's international reputation has led him to be sought after by the media. Such recognition becomes self-generating. Recently, his Milwaukee Art Museum building was put on the cover of the *Zoomorphic* book that worked like an exhibition catalogue for the Victoria and Albert Museum's autumn 2003 architecture exhibition on this theme. The question arises, should Calatrava's buildings be seen in this context or is the publisher banking on Calatrava's credibility to sell a dubious architectural concept?

Is It All About Image?

This page
Press Packs

These are press materials Peter Carzasty used to promote new facilities and buildings for high profile cultural organisations such as the Contemporary Art Museum in St Louis, Broadway's Symphony Space and the New 42nd Street Studios. Carzasty has developed a way to communicate with the culture sectors of the press as a result of his education. He has a Master of Fine Arts in Performing Arts Management. This led him to intern at a prestigious theatre festival in Williamstown, Massachusetts. Carzasty progressively got to know the players in the field. Through various stages, he became Director of Publicity and Public Relations at the Brooklyn Academy of Music and in 1993 started at Kreisberg Group where he led the campaign on the Rafael Viñoly designed Kimmel Center for the Performing Arts in Philadelphia

**Kimmel Center for
the Performing Arts Cuttings**

The author worked with Rafael
Viñoly architects' London
office when it opened in 2001
and subsequently collaborated
with Peter Carzasty on the
UK promotion of the Kimmel
Center for the Performing
Arts in Philadelphia. It is
not unsual for this type of
international PR collaboration
to take place on such major
projects and, in particular, with
American cultural institutions.
The help of a cuttings agency
such as the International
Press Cuttings Bureau
facilitates keeping track of
coverage

stories about a project. As a specialist in cultural PR, Carzasty describes his approach: 'I work contextually and always ask, what is the context in which a project is becoming public. Art centres are a dime a dozen. What differentiates one centre from others? Is it the design, its urban context, method of funding, or programming? How does this project relate to what is currently in the market place? If you don't know the context where one might fit you cannot advocate a project properly.'

Specialists will be aware of the latest media trends that might give rise to unexpected PR opportunities, as Carzasty describes, 'Court houses are increasing in both public and media popularity. Richard Meier is doing one in Long Island, Morphosis in San Francisco. They will get attention because they are the most democratic of all buildings'. It is true that such building types go through phases of popularity, particularly in the specialist design press. Recently, office buildings, renamed as workplaces, were 'the thing' to be writing about, yet as Carzasty says, much depends on the client and location of such a project. Looking across the Atlantic, he does feel that in Europe, as opposed to the United States, there is a desire to publish projects to which readers may not have access at all because of the inherent general knowledge of architecture overall. Again, only an experienced publicist would know how to work such a worldwide feel for media interest into a coherent strategy and PR campaign. However, this level of appreciation would be difficult to find in a non-specialist PR agency. As Carzasty says at the end of the interview, 'I am a stronger advocate knowing the nuances of the field.'

SHoP Architecture, New York

Laura Iloniemi

The approach to PR by New York-based SHoP/
Sharples Holden Pasquarelli is exemplary in the way
the practice has publicised its early work. It has led
not only to attracting bigger projects but also to the
type of client body that is taking the architects in the
direction they want to go as a design studio. The
practice is top-heavy with five partners looking over a
staff of ten. In PR terms this may not be ideal. Who is
the figurehead of the practice? In some practices one
of the senior partners often adopts this role for
various reasons from natural networking ability to
having writing and public speaking skills, or academic
and other credentials that help communicate the
work. The result may be a lopsided image of the
practice whereby, to the outside world, other partners
do not exist. Internally, this can cause tension.

At SHoP, the partners have divided the PR roles
within the practice in terms of who sits on boards,
who teaches and who looks after marketing and press
contacts. This has made the public relations
component more manageable for each partner and,
at the same time, allowed exposure for each partner.
Moreover, it has enabled the partners individually to
do the things they do best as well as have enough
time for clients and staff whilst being always involved
in the design of the projects at hand.

The key element in this type of approach to PR is
to ensure follow-up. Otherwise, all that networking
can far too easily go no further than, 'Guess who I
saw last night? We should really do something with
them'. SHoP is very aware of the need to look after
its contacts, and inform and nurture them like close
friends of the practice. Partner Kim Holden has taken
this challenge very much in her stride. Her strength
as a good promotional force for the practice is that

she is 'hands-on' and realises the value in what is
perhaps the less glamorous side of PR. 'You need to
be highly organised and appreciate the follow-up
required. Engage people. And back in the office get
out the materials required for publishers etcetera …
I can make things look polished. I am good at
tailoring a package to the recipient. We like to make
people feel special to us … We don't have formal
press releases … We work on case by case', Holden
explains.

It is true that PR works best when it is
personalised. It is very human to enjoy a handwritten
note, a phone call to come and see something, or
whatever invitation or reminder that shows the
enthusiasm the practitioners have for their projects.
Journalists, of course, like to think they are given an
exclusive preview. They often like the notion of
nurturing a practice from its early days and dealing
with the same people, especially the creators rather
than the promoters. The input at partner level is key
if only to provide the outward face for the public
relations whilst delegating behind the scenes work.

A difficulty arises when a back of house publicist
or member of administrative staff looking after the
practice's PR is not very experienced or familiar with
who is who. If this is the case, it is very difficult for
him or her to take an overview about who the
practice should be talking to and where they should
be seen. This is why Kim Holden vets all
correspondence and messages relating to publicity
such as lecture or publication requests and actions
these accordingly. She says this is as important as
the other things she does as an architect. Holden
is right to view PR in this way, especially as it is only
by doing this that one will make time for it.

Opposite
SHoP Partners
Kim Holden, the H in SHoP
says, 'There are five of us.
Together we cover more ground
in terms of contacts. At a party
there are five of you
networking at once'. From left
to right are partners William
Sharpless, Coren Sharpless,
Christopher Sharpless, Gregg
Pasquarelli and Kim Holden.
Kim Holden has a key role as
the PR engine for the practice.
She is charged with overseeing
the look and dissemination of
promotional materials. This
includes writing on the
projects. The other partners
are, as she says, 'Out there,
educating people about our
work, all of which has led to
an interest for people to go to
our projects and an elevated
interest in our work'. The
partners all also scout
international design
conferences and attend
lectures. This is a real
investment in taking part in
the world of architecture as a
whole, both intellectually and
in terms of profile. At an
overseas event, networking
opportunities are often easier.
People you cannot reach over
the phone are staying at the
same hotel, for instance, and
one can be informally
introduced to new, valuable
contacts

Right, top and bottom
SHoP, Me & Ro Jewellery
Store, NoLita, downtown
New York, 1999
'Small projects are critical to
get work', says Kim Holden,
and adds, 'This is why they
are still on our website'.
On the web, SHoP describe
Me & Ro: 'The design aimed
to create a space that was
powerful enough to draw
passers-by into the store,
without competing with the
delicacy of the small objects
in the showcases'. A similar
statement could be true of
a major exhibition design

Below left
SHoP, Museum of Sex,
New York, 2001
SHoP received the Progressive
Architecture Award for its
design for the Museum of
Sex. This was a turning point
for the practice in terms of
putting its name on the map.
The award is an opportunity
for young practices to get
recognised early on for unbuilt
work

Below right (top)
SHoP Intro Logo
on Website
Much has been made recently
of the names of architecture
practices. Sharples Holden
Pasquarelli has opted for a
hybrid solution of combining

an acronym with a word that
reflects what they are about.
Kim Holden says it is a
reference to the practice's
model shop, the notion of
the office being run like a
studio or of one-stop shopping
for clients. If a bit trendy in
terms of how big shopping
is as a leisure activity today,
the name is wonderfully
unpretentious too. It describes
the architect like a shop clerk,
humbly there to serve their
clients. Often art collectors
say of manicured white
walled galleries, 'I wish this
felt more like a shop less
like a museum'. Perhaps
Sharples Holden Pasquarelli
is responding to a desire to
demystify architecture.

Holden does say that with
acronyms there is, 'the danger
of alphabet soup', which is
why a word like SHoP (the
practice also played with
PUSH) helps glue it all together

Below right (bottom)
Still from Website
The SHoP website at
www.shoparc.com is
wonderfully easy to navigate.
The contact page makes
excellent use of the medium
by allowing a prospective
visitor to identify members
of the practice through
mug shots. This can be
very useful when trying to
remember who was who
at a meeting

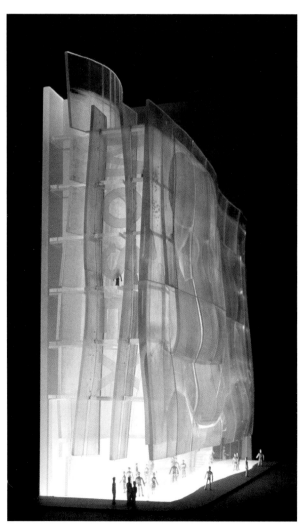

This page
SHoP, The A-Wall Trade Show Booth for *Architecture Magazine,* **New York, 2000**
Collaborations with magazines are excellent ways of ensuring one gets published and can be useful in building up long-term goodwill with an editorial team. In terms of profile, the endorsement of a critic as a client is always positive. A number of practices have benefited from being nurtured by certain publications or writers early on in their careers. For Alvar Aalto, the support of writer Morton Shand and *The Architectural Review* in London was essential to getting his work recognised overseas. SHoP has enjoyed the support of renowned American architectural cognoscenti such as Reed Kroloff, former editor of *Architecture Magazine*, and Philip Noble, an architectural historian who contributes to the *New York Times*, *Metropolis* and *Art Forum*

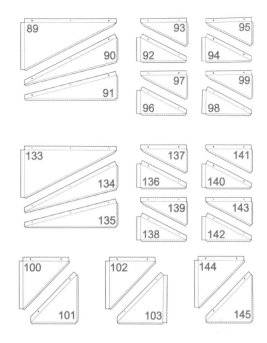

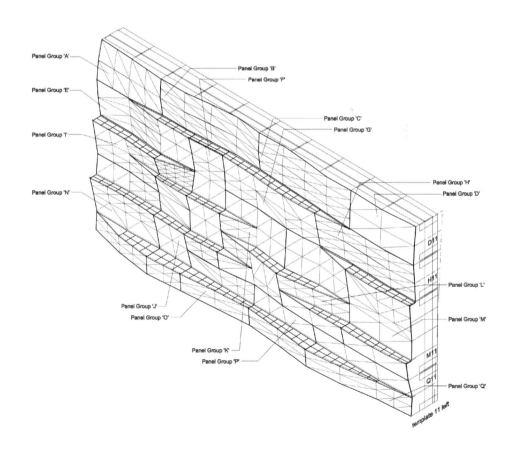

Opposite and right
SHoP, Porter House
Condominium, New York,
2003
Located in Manhattan's
Meatpacking District, the
Porter House Condominium
comprises of the conversion of
a six-storey warehouse into a
residential block for developers
Jeffrey M Brown Associates.
SHoP has created a pair of
daytime and nighttime visuals
to tell the story of the building.
Often this type of visual, or a
set showing buildings at
different seasons, can be very
compelling to the media as an
immediate graphic device for
'talking through images'

Overleaf
SHoP, Fashion Institute of
Technology, New York
The Fashion Institute of
Technology is located in the
heart of New York's fashion
scene. SHoP's design was
intended to create a shop
window for the institute, 'a
dynamic interaction between
the academy and the
professional world.' This is a
saleable concept that makes it
easy for clients and press alike
to understand the added value
that design can bring to project
by enhancing the perception
of an institution as an actively
outward-looking place

For SHoP, the proof is in the pudding. The practice's efforts in the realm of PR have paid off. Holden lists the benefits, 'People say it's refreshing to get things on time'. This results in exposure and the credibility it provides, 'We are passed being up and coming'. Being thorough and punctual with providing information may seem obvious, yet, I am convinced, one is halfway there in battling for exposure by just doing this. It is so rare.

In the realm of PR related activities, Holden cites SHoP's involvement in academia. A theory based approach, or some similar identifying direction, is key for the outside world to be able to categorise and understand where the practice is coming from. The importance of this kind of positioning of oneself is far too often underestimated. The ability to communicate the message of how the practice wants to contribute to the built environment regularly, and what it has done recently to achieve this, is actually paramount to getting noticed. As long as the presentation materials are good, projects do not need to be finished to achieve this. This is where SHoP caught on early by promoting methodologically what may now seem to the practice to be modest scale

projects such as the Costume National clothing store in Wooster Street, New York (1997); the Me & Ro jewellery store in the NoLita section of downtown New York (1999); and the A-Wall Trade Show Booth for *Architecture Magazine* (2000).

The PR tack was to promote these and other projects in such a way that it became clear that the ideas realised on these small-scale projects could work at a larger scale: ideas like custom design through mass production, and installations that could be made to work in a museum or park just as well as at a trade show.

Holden explains how the SHoP PR strategy is about, 'Using promotion to get the work rather than publicising built work for its own sake'. As a result, she says, 'By the time a project is built, a level interest is there and people are watching to see if it will work'. This drip-feed of interest throughout a project's life, compounded with a message about the practice ethos, has placed SHoP in the eye of the media in such a way that, 'We never have to beg to be published, we have been spoiled but would never take it for granted'.

Ocean North, Helsinki

Laura Iloniemi

In recent years, very young practices have been able to create a profile for themselves, which in the eyes of the more established firms may outweigh their experience in building. However, media exposure is not just about reporting what one has built. As Kivi Sotamaa of the Helsinki-based design studio Ocean North explains, 'Publishing ideas allows us to take part in the architectural debate; it creates an avenue for our work to be seen. Through publishing, a collective forum is made possible with our colleagues in the wider field'. This is important for Ocean North as it is a young practice that, as Sotamaa says, 'is not commercially driven but culturally so, to do ambitious work from the heart, always wanting feedback for our work'; he adds, 'we publish everything we do and thus make it available for open discourse and take part in it as well'. Sotamaa realises this is a way for a very small practice of only four people to protect its ideas and take ownership of them.

A large number of up and coming practices have used publicity for commercial ends. Getting known is about getting more credibility and thus, hopefully, more work. Ocean North has succeeded in doing what many practices dream of: getting known internationally, enabling the architects to work in Finland, Norway, the United Kingdom and also the United States, Italy and Estonia. This is a result of having Kivi and his partner Tuuli Sotamaa lead the Helsinki office with Birger Sevaldson in Norway and Michael Hensel in England.

It is true that by virtue of their physical presence in these countries, half the battle to get grounded is already won. Yet, it is not unusual for even very established, large practices with resident studios still to find it difficult to break into a new country. Ocean has benefited from having individuals *in situ* who really know the architectural culture of their countries and who are pushing the thinking in the design milieu that they are inhabiting.

For a small practice with modest PR resources, originality of thought is key, as is the ability to present its vision. Sotamaa knows that in Finnish architectural circles, which are very building oriented, a theory focused practice such as Ocean North is the odd one out. From a media perspective this is refreshing and Ocean North is regularly contacted to do interviews or features in the Finnish press. The fact that the practice is multidisciplinary and forges strong links with industrial design also makes its story attractive, as does its very experimental way of using digital technologies. Internationally, a Finnish practice of this type is also refreshing and appealing. It positions itself as a new direction in the legacy of Finnish Modernism.

This would suggest that for small practices it is essential to be clear about where they fit in the world of architecture if they are going to be noticed. Sotamaa says that in his experience, 'Architecture is unlike fashion in which stars can rise very quickly. The main thing in architecture', he points out, 'is that you have worked for a long time, been seen to be doing so regularly, and thus gradually create an impression'. Sotamaa believes that, 'In architecture people are seeking visionaries, accountability, and continuity'. He is wary of the current trend for trying to create a cult of superstars in architecture and Ocean North has consciously decided against the types of publicity that endorse this type of media attention.

Opposite
Ocean North
Set up in 1995, Ocean North emerged out of the Architectural Association's graduate design programme. It has been described as a non-Vitruvian formation of practice. This is due to its unconventional ways of running the studio from several places and being led by a desire for the exchange of ideas rather than single-handed authorship. There appears to be a delight in the flux of new inspiration, waves of influence that travel around the world. From left to right, Kivi Sotamaa, Tuuli Sotamaa, Birger Sevaldson and Michael Hensel

This page and overleaf
Ocean North, Formations Installation, commissioned by Fondazione Nicola Trussardi, Milan, 2002
This project exemplifies Ocean North's interest in the environment as a whole; architecture, interior design and product design merge in the installation at the Trussardi Gallery. The project and its visualisation are depictive of this approach that blurs the boundaries of different areas of design. In PR terms, it is ideal to be able to produce images that represent the core values of the design

Left and below
Ocean North, World Trade
Center Competition, New York,
2002–3
There is no doubt that small
practices can think big and
even get big exposure because
of it. Ocean North's entry for
the World Trade Center
competition was televised on
a Channel 4 programme
featuring the Venice
Architecture Biennale 2002.
The computer renderings
created by Ocean North for the
project are so sophisticated
that a number of the short-
listed entries' visuals pale in
comparison. The ability to use
computer graphics in an
innovative way that challenges
the reader is an area where
young creative teams can
really stand out. As Kivi
Sotamaa says, 'Our ability to
read computer visuals develops
the whole time. All of a
sudden you can recognise
what programme was used to
generate an image. We don't
use readily available drawing
packages at design concept
stage but look to animation
programmes used in, for
example, the film or military
industries.' Ocean North's
WTC entry was also picked up
by *Aftenposten* in Norway,
The Guardian and *Building
Design* in England as well
as the *New York Times*

OCEANNORTH

IONIC.NIFCA.ORG CREDITS
Initiator & Curator Rebecca Gordon Nesbitt / Nordic
Institute for Contemporary Art

Project co-ordinator Kivi Sotamaa / OCEANNORTH
Project technical co-ordinator Juha Huuskonen /
Olento + katasto.fi
Conceptual design Juha Huuskonen & Kivi Sotamaa
Design Kivi Sotamaa, Birger Sevaldson, Michael
Hensel, Kim B. Larsen ('project member') /
OCEANNORTH

Graphics Timo Helenius
Sound Ville Martin
Programming Juha Huuskonen, Arto Chydenius /
Olento + katasto.fi
Consultants Sumea rendering engine SUMEA Sami
Arola

We would also like to thank Minna Piirainen,
PLACEBO EFFECTS, HYBRID, Timo Aila, TAIKA
Technologies, Niko Punin, REMEDY, Jussi Rasanen,
Interactive Institute / KTH Tobi Schneidler

The project is commissioned and funded by NIFCA,
Nordic Institute for Contemporary Art

ionic.nifca.org

Ionic

Installations   Architecture   Exhibition Design   Urban   Objects   **Digital Design**
Projects   News   Events   Information

Left
Ocean North's Home Page
Ocean North's website at
www.ocean-north.net is
extremely user-friendly.
Navigation on the site never
leads you so deep that you
find yourself drowning when
trying to surface from surfing
through layers and layers of
information. Instead, the
navigation route is more linear,
allowing searches to take place
with minimum effort. One can
flick between general and more
specific information without
getting entangled or lost in
the 'sticky web' of information
overload. On project pages,
there is only essential text
information available for a
quick overview with the option
to read more, which again
allows for ease of browsing

Left and below
Ocean North, Finnish
Embassy, Canberra, 1997
Commercial international practices sometimes boast that they can keep their show running around the clock because drawings are worked on in New York once Europe stops and then picked up on in Australia. Ocean North used new communication technologies early on and has a well-established way of working on projects through a server that can be accessed by partners in Helsinki, Oslo and London. Yet Kivi Sotamaa says that doing things in person is still paramount and for him what has really made Ocean North a plausible international entity is the ease of flying to meet people. It is, therefore, not surprising that the practice's entry for the Finnish Embassy in Canberra has that same spirit of both local and global presence. The practice says, 'As inter- and trans-national corporations and institutions equal and bypass nation-states in degrees of general, public presence … the nation-state can revise its own terms … for servicing the public and its role in relationship to the distribution of politico-economic power'. To set the scene in these analytical terms, rather than in purely architectural ones, is to engage with the public about what design can achieve beyond its purely aesthetic or functional qualities

Top and bottom
Ocean North (Kivi Sotamaa, Tuuli Sotamaa and Michael Hensel), Exhibition Design for ARS **01 Unfolding Perspectives, commissioned by** KIASMA – **Museum of Contemporary Art Helsinki, Finland, 2001**
Kivi Sotamaa describes working with curators as an opportunity to engage clients with the theoretical thinking behind the architecture of the practice. Mostly, he feels clients are not interested in this side of the design but are more taken by a practice's attitude or signature. Working with a museum provides a good way to allow a practice to focus on its artistic ambitions whilst being seen by a variety of potential clients who are generally interested in the arts and design. Ocean North collaborated with the Museum of Contemporary Art Helsinki on an exhibition design for ARS 01. The exhibition design proved how the architects can engage the curatorial community by exploring arenas of new viewer experience. Ocean North did this by investigating a new relation between art and 'its hosting environment', making the latter an integral part of viewing exhibits

Is It All About Image?

Alsop Architects, London

Laura Iloniemi

Will Alsop's work thrives on image-making. His practice's images are always eye-catching, memorable, distinct and arty – just the sort of things that architectural writers want to cover. As a personality, Alsop is often described as an artist, an *enfant terrible*. This appeals to the media in much the same way it does in the art world with Damien Hirst or in the restaurant business with master chef Marco Pierre White. There is an image of a person who breaks the boundaries, who dares, who is creative. The media and general public have invested much in this type of cult of the artist; it is the secular society's response to attaining something profound, something beyond the mundane, practical and commercial. It adds colour, pizazz and awe to the everyday, grey, serious, business of building.

Alsop is aware of the academic constraints that keep many of his colleagues from adopting a colourful approach to how they present themselves or their work. He says, 'In architecture there is a tendency to say that, if it's academic, it must be okay.' At Alsop Architects, he prefers to, 'Discover what buildings want to be. Not theory.'

Such an explanation of the work is catchy, if vague. It immediately suggests that there is something more to the work than a building. In the case of Peckham Library by Alsop Architects there is. A whole area was lifted beyond belief by this single building.

Deborah Stratton's PR agency, Stratton Reekie, was appointed by Alsop Architects at the time of the Peckham Library project. Stratton Reekie was already a well-established PR firm that had worked with architects for a good 15 years. The agency's current roster of clients, in addition to Alsop Architects,

includes Robert Adam, Shepherd Robson and Lifschutz Davidson.

Alsop says that he decided to employ out-of-house PR consultants to look after the already existing number of press queries: 'These needed to be moderated, and handled strategically'. To this end, Stratton now meets with Alsop monthly. She describes Alsop as an exceptionally media-savvy client whose exposure has widened since having a co-ordinated PR approach and push by the her team. She describes Peckham Library as a good project for generating enormous media interest, 'It hit all the buzz words, regeneration, repositioning of a library, *enfant terrible*'.

At the PR meetings, Stratton and Alsop discuss what messages should be getting out there about the practice. 'Will will always have good suggestions.' However, it sounds as though Stratton Reekie's close liaison with the PRs of Alsop Architects' respective clients is key to successful campaigning, as is Stratton Reekie's overview of where projects are at in the practice and what potential highlights or milestones there might be in the course of a year. She does acknowledge, as is very often the case, that the trick is to get the information out of the practice.

Another important element in ensuring successful promotion of the work is Stratton Reekie's input on which images are used in the media. Stratton says that, 'Alsop Architects often create something to shock or to get a reaction with specific press images'. She says that the in-house illustrator team makes a huge contribution to the overall image of the practice.

It is certainly true that, as Stratton comments above, and Littlefield below (from the press point of view), Will Alsop is a media natural. His whole

'Our work as architects, currently poised to be able to give the world extraordinary objects of desire, is under threat by people who see the world as a dull and uncultured place of day to day tedium and boredom. STOP THEM. Write them out of your story.'

This page and overleaf
Alsop Architects, Peckham
Library, London, 2000
Projects such as the Library at Peckham were widely published. The publicity was boosted by the project winning the practice the Stirling Prize. Awards often are a good route for more media attention. Yet, in the case of Peckham, the crime rates in the area had kept it in the eye of the media. The Alsop sketches of projects such as the Peckham Library are clever in that they express the 'joy' that Will Alsop talks about when referring to his work. They are accessible to non-architects too

manner, and perhaps even his physique, suits this business of being a media persona. Yet, Alsop is very astute about the current state of affairs in the UK architecture media. He laments the loss of highly informed critics like Reyner Banham and the general lack of criticism: 'Current writers tend to be very ignorant ... Some only choose to write about stuff they are nice about.' Alsop describes a confusion between the role of journalists, critics and historians today. He says that the journalist tries to be a critic, the critic a historian and the historian a journalist, whereas someone should see it as their job to either report the news, give a considered reaction, or offer long term overview. An architect who is this eloquent about the media is ideally placed to gain exposure in the press. No wonder the media hunger for Alsop so much that, until recently, he was writing a weekly column in *The Architects' Journal* that, like it or not, held the reader's interest.

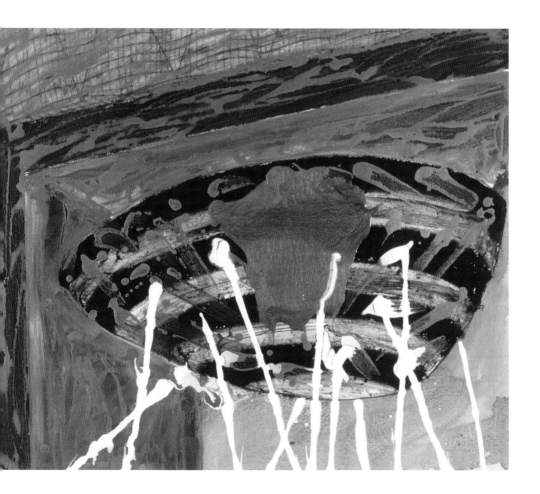

Profile of Will Alsop

David Littlefield
Former News Editor of *The Architects' Journal*

Will Alsop is a regular feature in the newspages of the architectural press; that's when he's not making a splash in the nationals or presenting his own television programmes. Of course, there is nothing like a catalogue of eye-catching buildings to get an architect noticed. Alsop certainly has that – notably in his Stirling Prize-winning Peckham Library, and North Greenwich tube station (designed and short-listed for the Stirling when Alsop was one third of Alsop Lyall & Störmer).

Alsop's practice is now extremely busy, but his media profile is hugely out of proportion to the workload. There are busier, and more exploratory, architects who struggle to make half the column inches Alsop does. To make the leap out of the professional press and into the nationals and broadcast media is no mean feat, but Alsop has managed it almost easily. He is a PR natural.

Alsop welcomes media attention. Although he employs a PR firm, he doesn't mind a direct approach from a journalist. In fact, when you meet him, he'll give you a card literally crammed with phone numbers, and if a journalist has to leave a message, they can be fairly sure he'll ring back. Alsop is fearless; he will be honest, mightily opinionated, talk off-the-record and use colourful language, which is why journalists like him. Getting a quote from Will Alsop will make an article more colourful.

As well as using words like 'beauty' and 'joy', language which most architects appear to find embarrassing, he also manages a neat turn of phrase. Describing his scheme for Barnsley as sufficient to turn it into a 'Tuscan hill town' was a stroke of genius – after that, none of the other architects recruited by Yorkshire Forward to rethink the area got a look in.

The practice's visuals are just as colourful. Rough sketches, design proposals and photorealistic CAD models all have a vibrancy that adds a dose of excitement to a page of editorial. Newspapers and magazines aren't obliged to publish worthy architectural schemes – from a publishing point of view, project illustrations in bold colours and daring compositions will make schemes far more tempting. Alsop realised this ages ago.

This page and opposite
**Alsop Architects, Fourth
Grace, Liverpool, 2008**
A much publicised project
on the newspages of trade
magazines, in particular,
the Fourth Grace project by
Alsop Architects offers the
exiting vision of Bilbao-esque
regeneration of Liverpool.
Matt Weaver described the
project in *The Guardian* on
21 November 2003, as,
'The futuristic "fourth grace",
the centrepiece of Liverpool's
successful bid to become the
European capital of culture
in 2008...'

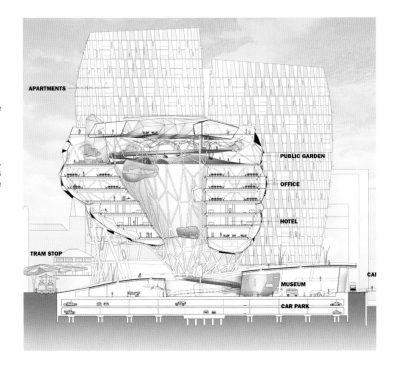

**Previous spread and below
Alsop Architects, Centraal
Masterplan, Rotterdam, 2002**
Listed playfully under 'Big
Architecture' on the Alsop
Architects website, this project
has unforgettable imagery.
In an article that begins, 'He
detests planners, thinks Bath
is boring and says his fellow
architects are "terrible people".
But why does Will Alsop, the
man behind some of Britain's
most exciting buildings, hate
Tate Modern?', Emma Brockes
of *The Guardian* (8 December
2003) tells readers about the
international profile of the
practice. 'Alsop has offices in
Rotterdam, Toronto, Singapore
and Shanghai, 120 staff in
all, a small outfit compared
to the mega-operations of
Norman Foster and Richard
Rogers, both of whom he beat
for the commission for the
Fourth Grace.' She continues,
'His real enemies are not
business rivals, but cultural
attitudes, which differ from
country to country. The Dutch,
for example, drive him crazy
with their fondness for
meetings. "You can end up,
literally, talking about whether
a building should be 10
centimetres to the left or
right – we're not outside
that danger in this country".'

Below

Alsop Architects, Hotel du Departement Des Bouches du Rhone, near Marseilles, 1994 The building was conceived to relocate the Departmental headquarters from the centre of Marseilles to the suburb of St Just as part of a regeneration initiative. The practice explains where it stands in terms of the design of the project: 'The impact of the building as a public landmark is vastly enhanced by the use of strong colour in the external elevations – stimulating, comfortable and affordable, the Hotel is the anthisesis of the conventional bureaucratic fortress.' This type of approach is keeping with the Will Alsop line of publicly denouncing accountants, management consultants and civil servants as a rather too pragmatic bunch

Prima donnas
Parties
Profile
Practice
Poetics
Patronage

The case studies on individual projects, from country houses to major commissions such as the World Trade Center Competition in New York, and small-scale ones like the Dorma Door Handle Design Commission, reveal how image is important in selling an idea to a potential client. The London Millennium Bridge article explores how a potential PR crisis – the wobbly bridge – can be assuaged by intelligent handling of the issues at hand, while the Melbourne Federation Square piece tackles the sensitive ground where PR is required to salvage a project from political death. The Dutch Scene article tells us how a country's cultural policies can get contemporary architecture to flourish at home and as an export. Much of the PR focus for all these examples is about pushing new ideas in order to deliver better projects; making the public aim higher in terms of design; and ensuring recognition for work well done while sometimes even doing a little spinning in order to beat off competition.

Project Case Study
Grafton New Hall, Cheshire

Laura Iloniemi

The Grafton New Hall Country House competition was the brainchild of developer Mel Hood of Ferrario Burns Hood, a company based in Cheshire and south Manchester that specialises in luxury housing developments in the area. Hood bought a 114-acre site which, in the early 17th century, was the location of Grafton New Hall. A private country house, it was described at the time as representing the new domestic architectural tendencies of the era, thus departing from the more fortified medieval residential building of previous centuries. After passing through the hands of several families, Grafton New Hall fell into disrepair in the 20th century and was demolished in 1963.

The plan to build a contemporary version of the old country house – the New Grafton New Hall as it were – was not without its difficulties. The planning guidance policy in England required that such a private dwelling development would need to be 'architecturally outstanding' in its design to be granted approval under the PPG7 legislation. Hood sought the advice of local planning consultants and architects on how to go about realising his vision for a 21st century country house in Britain. As a result, in the spring of 2001, the route of organising an architectural competition that would attract the best practices was decided upon. This was done in close collaboration with the Royal Institute of British Architects (RIBA) and with eminent figures such as Spencer de Grey, a senior partner at Foster and Partners, consulting on the process.

The entire process was newsworthy: a commercial developer investing in the best of what the United Kingdom's designers had to offer in order to sell his idea of modern living to the ultra-rich – the new

landowners (the price tag for the New Grafton Hall was quoted as high as £20 million). In England, the notion of designing what would be an avant-garde country house was, at that time, a novel and fresh idea. It offered an original way to look at what was customarily a traditional world and, thus, made for a reinvention story, a reappraisal story of who are the new country gentry. Certainly, speculation on the potential client for this type of house whetted journalists' appetites. There we have it: architect or design concept aside, Grafton New Hall as a story had so many things going for it that it would guarantee some media mileage.

In the summer of 2001, the RIBA design competition for Grafton New Hall was won by Ushida Findlay, a smallish practice that had excellent design pedigree and international recognition – its work had been published in the Spanish 2G monographic magazine series by the prestigious Barcelona-based Gustavo Gili editorial house. The practice had a portfolio of exquisite projects in Japan and, at around the time of the Grafton New Hall competition, Kathryn Findlay of Ushida Findlay had opened an office in Shoreditch, East London. Her reputation of having been 'big in Japan' certainly opened doors in London but, as a designer Ushida Findlay was not a household name by any stretch of the imagination. The winner for Grafton New Hall was selected purely on the basis of the architecture and not on media credentials. Very refreshing!

After the summer, attentions focused on developing and launching the winning design. However, the originally planned launch date of autumn 2001 was delayed for two reasons. Firstly, the designs as evolved by the architects required

revisiting in order to fulfil the developer's vision for the project. Secondly, the tragedy of 11 September made it questionable to promote the sale of a luxury property later that year. Following consultation with my own company, Laura Iloniemi Architectural Press and PR, who had been appointed to promote Grafton New Hall on behalf of Ferrario Burns Hood, a New Year date for going public on the Grafton New Hall designs was decided upon.

Until the Grafton New Hall designs were unveiled on 12 February 2002, Ushida Findlay's coverage had been primarily in the design press which had picked up on the visually very compelling work of the practice. Ushida Findlay's buildings, due to their truly unique approach and eye-capturing forms, had become coveted by publications such as *Domus* and *Architectural Review*. Kathryn Findlay had also received coverage in the Scottish national newspapers as she is a 'local girl made good', in addition to some coverage revolving around women architects. Yet, nothing major had been published in the UK national newspapers until Grafton New Hall was launched. Then the success was phenomenal. Jackson Stops, who acted as sales agents for the Grafton New Hall property, had never had a property attract so much coverage. Jackson Stops's PR consultant Margie Coldrey of MCPR proved to be a very valuable asset, adding to the mix of property and architecture contacts that were being made aware of Grafton New Hall.

The coverage included warm-up pieces in the *Financial Times* (Business Supplement, 2 February 2002), *The Sunday Times* (20 January 2002), *Evening Standard* (26 November 2001), *The Spectator* (24 November 2001) and *Country Life* (31 January 2001), and, after the unveiling of the design, major features in the *Financial Times* (13 February 2002 and Weekend FT 16–17 February 2002), *The Times* (13 February 2002), *The Guardian* (13 February 2002), *The Independent* (13 February 2001; 21 February 2001), *Daily Mail* (13 February 2001), *The Spectator* (16 March 2001), and a *Country Life* editorial (28 February 2001), not to mention local press interest all along. Subsequent press included the *Financial Times* ('How To Spend It' supplement, 2 March 2002, and Weekend FT, 29–30 June 2002), *The Guardian* (13 April 2002), *Telegraph* magazine (18 May 2002), *Sunday Telegraph* (10 February 2002, 31 March 2001), *The Independent* (25 May 2002) and others.

The advertising value of the coverage in the dailies alone on the day of the launch would be worth approximately £170,000 using current rates. All the articles, except a couple of tongue in cheek local Manchester paper headlines, were very positive and supportive of the avant-garde design. The architectural correspondents heralded Grafton New Hall as:

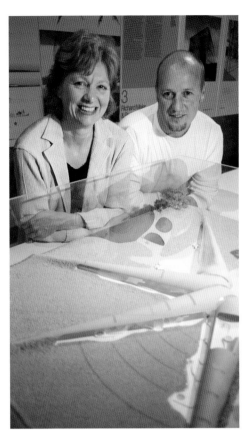

'Modernists triumph over traditionalists with radical design for Cheshire mansion'. Anne Spackman, *Financial Times*

'Ushida Findlay have plainly created something extraordinary'. Jay Merrick, *The Independent*

'Grafton New Hall is a remarkable attempt to redefine a form of domestic architecture'. Jonathan Glancey, *The Guardian*

'A starfish-shaped mansion is set to catapult the concept of the English country house into the 21st century'. Valerie Elliott, *The Times*

'A characteristically radical design that has little time for the classical tradition and a lot of time for the landscape'. Robert Bevan, *Building Design*

It was true, the starfish-shaped design that Kathryn Findlay and her team had come up with had made an immediate impact. The resemblance to a recognisable sea-creature form certainly appealed to people's imaginations, as did the potential for envisioning a James Bond-like *séjour* in the house as designed by Ushida Findlay. In this way, the

architects have in the end very much lived up to creating what their client Mel Hood had hoped for – a truly memorable and even tantalising piece of architecture. Ushida Findlay had done this whilst also securing planning permission for the project. What is more, true to their organic design ethos, Kathryn Findlay and her team ensured the building adapted well to its surroundings by embracing the landscape, rather than dominating it in the way former country houses had done. This is more than superficially true because the building is inherently environmentally friendly as it adopts sustainable building practices.

In the press releases that first announced Ushida Findlay as the winner of the Country House Competition, particular attention was paid to not selling the project as just 'another pretty face' or, as architects would say, a statement or signature building. Instead, the release sold the project for its real merits: a new look at country living; a gutsy approach to development; and a design that offers a real contribution to architectural history and the understanding of a building type, the country house. No images were released of the Grafton New Hall design with the first release. Instead reference images of other Ushida Findlay work were included to indicate what was on offer.

THE WINNER OF THE NEW MODERN COUNTRY HOUSE THE ROYAL INSTITUTE OF BRITISH ARCHITECTS (RIBA) COMPETITION IS ANNOUNCED

The country house is back, but not as you know it ... Imagine a substantial and ultra modern Hall that breaks with the tradition of dominating the landscape and instead, reflects and positively embraces nature. At the same time, an organic feel will offer an alternative to the tired old townie cliché of minimalism. The design for this house evolved from a competition organised by the prestigious Royal Institute of British Architects and won by esteemed architects Ushida Findlay.

The concept for the New Modern Country House project came from the developers Ferrario Burns Hood (FBH). Mel Hood of FBH who originally initiated the staging of the RIBA competition, says:

'The competition was a unique opportunity to see how Britain's best architects interpret modern living. At Ferrario Burns Hood, we feel privileged to be working with the winning team Ushida Findlay who we know will make our vision of the 21st century country house as a contemporary work of art come true.'

Traditionally, England's country houses have been defined by a very formal understanding of decorum. The recent renewed interest in country houses has been led by wealth generated by the creative economies. Ushida Findlay's design marks a transition towards catering for this wider and more international client circle with an approach fed by the demands of a more modern lifestyle. For these clients, the urban retreat is a microcosm of their own world, as opposed to a social status symbol. Ushida Findlay's interpretation of the building type will thus no doubt be an important step in the history of the English country house.

The Estate Agents for the Modern Country House project are Jackson-Stops & Staff. Crispin Harris Director at Jackson-Stops & Staff describes the property and what it holds in store for the prospective buyer,

'The sheer scale of a new 25,000 square foot avant-garde country house within an expanse of over 100 acres of land is in itself exciting. Yet for us, this project is unprecedented in truly offering new ground to country living and art appreciation.'

Despite advances in architectural design, the underlying reasons for owning a country house remain unchanged. The appreciation of nature, peace and cleanliness are luring more and more urbanites to seek sanctuary, and in turn, actively support the preservation of rural areas. This respect for the environment is reflected in Ushida Findlay's organic approach to design. Much attention is paid to light, air, acoustics, health, and the quality of life as well as the positive integration into the local ecology and community.

Moreover, most people would agree that, for the contemporary country house to be successful, it needs to respond to today's way of life. Ushida Findlay's design is exclusive and sophisticated but at the same time both energy efficient and sustainable. Facilities meet the requirements of modern living discreetly and preferably without the aid of staff.

For Kathryn Findlay of Ushida Findlay, the project of designing the New Modern Country House is about looking forwards, creating milestones, in the way past architects have done. She says,

'We think of the project as a laboratory for new design models specially created for the Modern Country House.'

There are of course strong historical precedents for this way of thinking. In fact looking back, Paxton's Great Conservatory at Chatsworth House represents a major achievement in the creation of building spaces to house 'artificial climates', and consequently led to the construction of Crystal Palace. Hardwick Hall marks a shift in the appearance of the country house from the residential to the domestic, from a public to private, with a main façade that has a high glazing-to-wall proportion.

To date, Ushida Findlay's design has integrated a Japanese understanding of form/materials and their relationship to nature. The design for the Kasahara Amenity Hall, Japan, is derived from the sun's path, creating a passive solar system which responds to each season. The thatched roof at The Poolhouse, in South England alludes to both Japanese and English craftsmanship.

The mail out of the first release resulted in some coverage announcing the competition winner but it was really meant to prepare the editors for lining up interviews and space (very important for long lead glossy publications) well in advance of the launch. It was also intended to set the tone for the coverage which, when comparing the quotations extracted above to the copy we produced, seems to have worked. (The release Laura Iloniemi Architectural Press and PR prepared for the property and design press is reproduced here. A slightly altered, more trend-conscious version was sent to consumer and lifestyle media.)

The very morning the press notice arrived, the property editor of the *Financial Times* wanted to be briefed on the project. Subsequently, similar one-to-one briefings were arranged with the leading property and architectural writers of other national papers with the architect, developer and agent. The idea was to drum up interest and secure coverage in the national newspapers prior to the day of the unveiling of the design. This unveiling, or design launch, was really organised to create momentum around revealing this mystery project as well as to ease the management of non-national media press interest. Those national media representatives granted special briefings prior to the launch were given embargoed images and the others were either biked images on the day or given them at the launch party. This ensured coverage on the day and the week of the launch.

This takes us to the topic of launching. Whether for a design unveiling, as in the case of Grafton New Hall, or another type of occasion, such as the opening of a building, a launch provides a good focus for a PR activity. Yet, one must not give too much away, for example, by revealing the design, or few will come. On the other hand, one must somehow also ensure the event has been pre-sold as something worth coming to well-in-advance. As a part of the Grafton New Hall campaign, Laura Iloniemi Architectural Press and PR sent out a press release in November 2001 that ensured some early warm-up publicity to get a word-of-mouth effect going about the building. This was followed by invitations to the launch in January 2002, with a more informative press release sent in good time prior to the event in order to get it into busy London diaries. The objective was also to activate the media before Christmas so that it was already on their agendas in the New Year, taking into account how quickly February comes around after the Christmas holidays. Timing and reminders to the press – without overkill – are everything.

The Grafton New Hall launch was a lavish affair held at the Hempel Hotel in London. Ferrario Burns Hood organised for champagne and canapés. Spencer de Grey was invited to say a few words at the unveiling of the screening of a computer fly-through DVD made by Virtual Planit, followed, as the *pièce de resistance*, by a physical model exhibiting the design in three dimensions – finally! There were over 50 members of the design and lifestyle press attending this daytime event in the midst of their fully packed schedules, deadlines and numerous other previews, PR luncheons and briefings for that week. A real buzz surrounded the occasion. Mobile phones rang and sang with those stuck at their desks wanting quotes from the developers, the architects and the agents.

Upon leaving, the guests to the launch were handed thick brochures on Grafton New Hall with plans and images of the model as well as copies of the DVD they had just been shown. Releases were worked down to a basic fact sheet that did not go overboard on blurb.

Created by Madhouse, the Grafton New Hall brochures were entitled 'A journey through space and time'. They were intended for potential buyers of the house but designed in such a way that they worked well as press materials, too. In fact, Jay Merrick of *The Independent* (21 February 2002) devoted quite a few column inches to the sales brochure and marketing concept of this entire enterprise. This is really a compliment to all of the Grafton New Hall team even though Merrick's remarks are teasing, 'You're looking at virtual architecture that, regardless of its potential physical and practical worth, is already medallioned with the kind of hype designed – highly designed – to ensure that nothing becomes something. Grafton New Hall has sprung into existence fully formed, but only in the mind. It may not be completed for years, but what does that matter? It's already out there.' Of the brochure, he writes, 'On the right-hand page – like the others, thick coated card more than a foot square – is a beautifully printed sans-serif text in grey that fits the space perfectly. Everything is obviously under control. No point in having an expensive idea unless it looks like an expensive big idea'.

Other journalists focused their stories, as can be gleaned from the above-cited quotations, on marvelling at the whole concept behind this undertaking in terms of what it says about commissioning architecture, what is the potential of seeing architecture as art, and what the future of top-end housing could hold. However, there is no doubt that the continuing stories came rolling off the keyboards of journalists as a result of a well-orchestrated PR campaign and design launch. The party for unveiling the design truly had the feeling of a big celebration rather than that of a product launch. It welcomed all to join in the fun of doing such an exciting project while thanking them for their goodwill. The PR effort itself did not go unnoticed. The *Telegraph* magazine said that the, 'unveiling was greeted with rapture by the press.'

Casa sperimentale nel Cheshire

ABITARE

419

INTERIORS DESIGN ARCHITECTURE ARTS

LUGLIO-AGOSTO/JULY-AUGUST 2002   € 6,70 (Italy only)   UK £ 9.50 - USA $12.00 - Can. $17.00

Case per il mare case per il sole

Kaufmann e Norlander:
piccole case prefabbricate

Svizzera Expo.02:
Coop Himmelb(l)au, Jean Nouvel,
Diller & Scofidio, Multipack

Proposte giovani e tutte le novità
dal Salone del Mobile 2002

Arte e fotografia

EXPERIMENTAL HOUSE IN CHESHIRE, ENGLAND - HOUSES FOR SEA AND SUNSHINE
KAUFMANN AND NORLANDER: SMALL PREFABRICATED HOUSES - SWITZERLAND EXPO.02:
COOP HIMMELB(L)AU, JEAN NOUVEL, DILLER & SCOFIDIO, MULTIPACK - YOUTHFUL IDEAS
AND ALL THE NEW PRODUCTS FROM SALONE 2002 - ART AND PHOTOGRAPHY

Millennium Bridge, London

David Littlefield

London's Millennium Bridge should have been a public relations dream. The 330 metre 'Blade of Light' – a collaborative effort between Architect Norman Foster, sculptor Sir Anthony Caro and Engineers Arup – was both an extraordinary object and the first new Thames crossing in London for a century. However, without knowing it, on the cusp of the millennium the design team, as well as Southwark Council and the Millennium Bridge Trust, still had more than two years hard graft ahead of them.

The bridge didn't open on Millennium Eve, but six months later on 10 June. Its opening was eagerly anticipated and 150,000 people descended on the bridge in three days, during which it developed the infamous wobble that forced its closure. Arup was soon to develop some new engineering terminology – 'synchronous lateral excitation' – and be plunged into a media frenzy that was unprecedented in the history of the company.

Fortunately, subsequent events have shown that a quick and honest response, and a genuine desire to engage with a hungry media, ensured that Arup survived this unhappy period with its reputation intact and even enhanced. It is now doing more bridge design work than ever before.

At the time, though, Arup media relations manager Harriett Hindmarsh felt almost overwhelmed with the media attention, which was being generated worldwide. 'Some of it was quite aggressive; we'd never had that level of attention. The volume of calls and the intensity of it was phenomenal', she says.

Even though the design team and its sponsors quickly decided that any planned approach to the media would be collectively agreed in advance, most of the PR work fell to Hindmarsh because, no matter where the actual blame for the problem lay, only Arup had the ability to discover the source of the problem and deal with it. This responsibility became even more pressing after Norman Foster consented to an interview with the *Evening Standard*'s Rowan Moore on 12 June in which he said the wobble was an engineering problem. Interestingly, this left Foster, who has said he was misquoted, open to further criticism; many in the media were scornful of the apparent way he was claimed to take credit for the bridge in advance of its opening only to melt into the background once the extent of the problem became evident.

Nonetheless, the charge appeared to stick. Arup quickly convened a series of crisis meetings and Hindmarsh agreed with Arup chairman Bob Emmerson and project director Tony Fitzpatrick that honesty was the best policy, even if they didn't know the answers (which, at first, they didn't). Hindmarsh has lost count of the number of times she patiently explained to journalists that, although there was obviously a problem, there was no obvious cause. Consequently, neither was there an obvious solution.

Tony Fitzpatrick was quickly immersed in media training to enable him to speak convincingly and concisely to a press which was little used to reporting engineering detail. This training was crucial because Hindmarsh felt it was important for the problem-solving team to have a clearly identifiable focus and, in spite of the strategy of absolute honesty, Fitzpatrick needed to professionalise his act. 'Tony had the sort of personality that would lead him to wax lyrical, but you only get a 30 second slot to get your soundbite across', says Hindmarsh.

Opposite and previous page
At the time of its opening, the
Millennium Bridge represented
both engineering and PR
challenges. It was originally
scheduled to open in time for
the New Year celebrations of
2000. When it finally opened
the following summer,
150,000 people crossed the
bridge in three days, resulting
in 'Synchronous lateral
excitation' and the
bridge's closure. Newspapers
led with headlines such as
'London Bridge is Closing
Down' and 'Bridge Over
Troubled Water'. The *Evening
Standard* even began a
'Reopen the Wobbly Bridge'
campaign when its closure
looked liked being a lengthy
one. A PR campaign based on
honesty and giving journalists
access to technical data
eventually led to positive
relations between the design
team and the media. When

the bridge finally reopened
on 22 February 2002,
pictures were broadcast
around the world

P 98–9
The bridge nears
completion, before the
wobble forced its closure
and the addition of 90
5-metre-long dampers.
The answer to the question
over who actually paid
for the remedial work has
remained a closely guarded
secret

Prior to the opening of the bridge, much had been
made of its daring design. Ordinarily, suspension
bridges are characterised by cables hung from tall
masts; nobody had attempted to design such a
shallow suspension bridge before. Exhaustive wind
tests had shown that the bridge should withstand
freak gales, unlike the Tacoma Narrows suspension
bridge in the USA that shook to destruction in 1940.

By the end of June, just two weeks after Arup had
controversially insisted on the bridge's closure in order
to conduct tests, the team had figured out what was
wrong. A press conference was convened on 28 June
at Arup's head office in London, and more than 60
journalists and camera crews from news organisations
from around the world turned up. In a sensible piece
of image-making, Norman Foster appeared shoulder-
to-shoulder with Tony Fitzpatrick, who admitted to
being 'embarrassed, but not ashamed'.

Foster used the press conference to respond to
the allegations of distancing himself, saying, 'We have
all in our own ways put our reputations on the line'.

Fitzpatrick revealed the swaying was caused by
'synchronous lateral excitation', a consequence of
large numbers of pedestrians falling into step with
each other in response to the natural movement of
the bridge. The huge numbers crossing the bridge
exacerbated this otherwise harmless movement,
causing the bridge to sway sickeningly. At this stage,
the team was honest enough to admit that it was too
early to define the solution, but that additional
dampers were likely.

Hindmarsh says the discovery of the cause of the
wobble created a PR conundrum; the science had to
be simplified for a non-technical media without giving
rise to expectations that there would be a quick and
simple solution. The research had to be dumbed-
down, but not too much. Hindmarsh is still not sure
that the right balance was struck – some newspapers
reduced the science even further to a sarcastic 'the
wrong kind of walking'.

After the source of the wobble had been identified
the media found other reasons to tenaciously hold
onto the story. On 29 June the *Evening Standard*'s
Simon Jenkins wrote an article entitled 'Give us our
Bridge Back – wobble or not'. Journalists were also
keen to know who was to pay for remedial work,
which was the subject of a confidentiality agreement
between the design team and its clients – it still is. To
this day it has never been reported which party, or
parties, paid for the work, which is an exemplary act
of group responsibility. In the latter half of 2000,
though, journalists' enquiries continued to pour in.

Hindmarsh had to build bridges of her own. She
formed close links with the *Evening Standard*, one of
the bridge's most vehement critics, and London
broadcasters. She provided exclusive information
about progress on the research, and access to tests
and the engineers themselves.

Arup's engineers worked closely with academics
from three universities throughout the summer. On 3

February 2002, *The Sunday Times'* architecture critic Hugh Pearman quoted an Arup engineer who had told him, 'We wrote the equivalent of three or four PhDs in the space of a few weeks'. By September the engineers had reached a solution, which was handed over to the Millennium Bridge Trust in three mighty volumes, each the size of a large encyclopaedia. By November, the Trust had agreed to the suggestion of retro-fitting 90 five-metre long dampers to the underside of the bridge to soak up unwanted motion. The idea was announced to the media after reducing the three-volume research into an eight-page document, and further into a one-page press release. Furthermore, a computer-generated video was created, taking viewers on a virtual reality tour of the bridge to show that the changes would have a minimal impact on the structure's clean lines. The video was shown world-wide.

Once the dampers had been installed, the bridge was ready for testing. In the run-up to the reopening on 22 February 2002, 800 Arup staff walked over the bridge. In spite of the fact that it was still officially closed, nobody noticed. Then 2000 people were invited to do the same thing – staff, pupils from the City of London School and employees from local businesses – and it became a media event. Thankfully, the wobble had disappeared.

Arup has emerged from the Millennium Bridge debacle remarkably well. Despite having never encountered a similar problem, the practice harnessed its virtues of honesty and collaborative learning with considerable success, both in terms of engineering and PR. In fact, its image is arguably stronger because of the company's proven ability to both tackle innovative structures and sort things out when they don't go quite according to plan.

Importantly, Arup has used the experience to inform work on future projects. A dedicated website, set up to cover the crisis and provide coverage of progress, puts detailed information firmly into the public realm. This was 'an excellent bit of public relations for the firm, and more importantly for

World Trade Center, New York

Will Jones with Laura Iloniemi

The international competition to design a new development and memorial alongside the World Trade Center Ground Zero site is a unique one from a PR perspective. Firstly, the media value of the 9–11 tragedy was such that there was immediately an interest in stories associated with the site and the response to the grief and damage caused by the terrorist attack. Alex Garvin, former vice president for planning, design and development at the Lower Manhattan Development Corporation, said that he had never witnessed this level of media interest in architecture. Secondly, the element of a race between the short-listed designs selected from over 400 entries in the competition, which then led to two finalists – the Think Team led by Rafael Viñoly and Studio Daniel Libeskind – created a drama that very easily allowed for favourites based on not only designs, but also personality. This latter element, in particular, made the promotional side of the competition unusual. It appeared that the finalists needed to gauge how to appeal not only as designers but as public figures. To some, this may seem a wholly unacceptable position. What other than the actual designs could be relevant for choosing the best team for the job?

It is clear from the reactions of some the short-listed practices that there was indeed profound disbelief in the value that playing up to the media and other types of political lobbying had in making an impact. Both Norman Foster and Richard Meier, who were in the final seven design teams short-listed for the project, relied on either just pushing the architectural concept or their reputation. The Foster team had produced some of the best visuals and were able to get these widely published. Perhaps this helped the UK-based practice, with its design for a pair of 'kissing towers', in becoming popular. Two polls, conducted by the New York Post and CNN at the time of the unveiling of the competition entrants, revealed that the public's initial favourite was in fact Foster. Richard Meier said of the media scrum surrounding the project: 'We didn't promote. We thought it was about the work, not promotion. We didn't behave the way that some others did; it is not in the personality of our team. And it showed in the fact that we didn't get chosen'. Others, like, Gregg Lynn of the United team (Foreign Office Architects, Gregg Lynn of FORM, Ben van Berkel and Caroline Bos of UN Studio) said: 'We were seriously behind in targeting the right people and getting across to the decision makers. If we'd had half a brain we'd have called up Hugh Hardy [of New York Visions] and trotted down to his office and explained our design to him!'

By comparison, these teams and others following the World Trade Center site competition coverage would probably agree that the Think Team and Studio Daniel Libeskind were media savvy. I (Laura Iloniemi) worked with Rafael Viñoly's London office to promote the Think Team's design in the UK. It seemed that the Think Team was never as quick on its feet to use the designer's persona or spend time on media interviews as its immediate competitor. Too often, architects' PR strategies are reactive in this way. It reflects the way PR is seen more as a last resort by most practitioners rather than as a pivotal tool in a campaign to win a job. Daniel Libeskind is good at PR perhaps through an innate talent for it or by recognising its importance. Libeskind seized the power of personality in some of the early statements about his practice's World Trade Center Study: 'I arrived by

ship to New York as a teenager, an immigrant, and like millions of others before me, my first sight was the Statue of Liberty and the amazing skyline of Manhattan. I have never forgotten that sight or what it stands for. This is what this project is all about.'

The emotional, pro-American pitch, if somewhat more sentimental than we are used to hearing from architects, is a much more accessible way to engage and explain one's approach than a similar extract from the Think Team's opening lines describing their project, 'Today creativity is based on the exchange and processing of information that is produced globally. The urban condition that up to now has hosted the process of innovation needs to be transformed into a spatial and sociological environment where this new kind of creativity can interact in a more global dimension.'

Similar differences in pitch echoed throughout the way in which the two finalists appeared in public. Studio Libeskind was always a step ahead in the stakes of street credibility. Libeskind's penchant for leather jackets and cowboy boots was noted in *Time* magazine. The finalists' glasses were even discussed in the *New York Times* by Ruth La Ferla, 'With their soaring towers and memorials, both concepts were the talk of the town. A few New Yorkers, however, seemed almost as impressed by the architects' eyewear. Mr. Viñoly appeared in photographs wearing two pairs of spectacles on his head – something of a fashion signature.'

In the same article New York architect Brian Sawyer is quoted saying 'Libeskind's glasses are out of control'. La Ferla explains 'He knows that for architects, signature glasses can be a conscious attempt to trademark their faces, much as they trademark a building. Mr Libeskind's frames are a particularly severe example of so-called statement glasses, meant to confer a degree of gravitas, but hinting all the while that he (or she) has raffishly artistic leanings.'

This type of media jousting is commonplace in the US, its highlight being the televised debates between candidates at presidential elections. In fact, the two teams grasped the political nature of the project perfectly, playing straight to the public as if the citizens of New York were the direct clients for the job. Julie Iovine of the *New York Times* reported: 'With talk of truth and beauty, memory and monument, these architects have been selling themselves like movie stars'. Robert Ivy, editor of *Architectural Record* observed, 'Usually it is the client in the lead orchestrating the media and managing the political situation. But, in the absence of a strong client and with an ad hoc political entity acting as developer, this unenviable task has fallen to the architects.'

Previous page
Shigeru Ban, Ken Smith, Frederic Schwartz, Rafael Viñoly, World Cultural Center – World Trade Center Competition Entry, New York, 2003
The Think Team's proposal for the 'World Cultural Center' included Rafael Viñoly, Frederic Schwartz, Shigeru Ban and Ken Smith. The team's entry was for two frameworks interspersed with cultural buildings and spaces. Rafael Viñoly said: 'This is a great moment for architecture. It's gone from being marginal to a way to truly regenerate the city's pride.'

Is It All About Image?

Right
Foster and Partners, Kissing Towers – World Trade Center Competition Entry, New York, 2003
Foster and Partners 'Kissing Towers' design for the World Trade Center site was an initial favourite with the New York public. The image was easy to understand and often the visual of the pair set against a warm sunny sky was used in the media. It was not unlike the typical postcard image of the original Twin Towers, thus creating an uplifting feel to the 'after' image

Below
Richard Meier, World Trade Center Competition Entry, New York, 2003
Richard Meier's WTC design was never in the final run. Many believed the American practice would have a good chance but the World Trade Center Competition, and all the issues around it, were considered very much from a global perspective. This was reflected in the short-list of architects

(1.)   THE HEART AND THE SOUL:
        MEMORY FOUNDATIONS

MEMORIAL SITE EXPOSES
GROUND ZERO
ALL THE WAY DOWN TO THE
BEDROCK FOUNDATIONS.

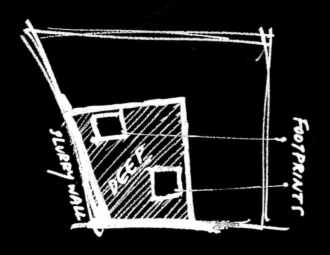

REVEALING THE HEROIC FOUNDATIONS
OF DEMOCRACY FOR ALL TO SEE.

Studio Daniel Libeskind, Memory Foundations – World Trade Center Competition Entry, New York City, 2003

Opposite
'Revealing the heroic foundations of democracy for all to see'. Daniel Libeskind's simple yet emotive sketch of the WTC site

Below
The Statue of Liberty at the foreground of this image sends a powerful message by relating the Libeskind design to the notion of freedom. The very name of the practice's scheme, 'Memory Foundations', is also compelling to the general public as are those of its components, 'Freedom Tower' and 'Wedge of Light'

Is It All About Image?

Opposite
Louis Hellman cartoons
Louis Hellman's cartoons
of Norman Foster (top) and
Daniel Libeskind (bottom)
pre-date the World Trade
Center Competition, making
it even more amusing to see
that he had named Foster
'The Untouchable' and
Libeskind 'The Contender'

However, the real question is, would any amount of this unprecedented media exposure, pontificating and posturing make a difference to the decision-makers? Had the PR push on behalf of the finalists paid off? I asked Alex Garvin this question when he spoke at the Royal Society of Arts in London. Had the creation of a persona, the charisma of the final two swayed the decision-makers? The answer was a flat and adamant 'no'; the issues at hand were, according to Garvin, way beyond being flung by the fancies of the media. Yet, the teams had invested real time and money in promoting their projects.

In his BBC programme 'Towering Ambition', Dan Cruickshank points out how politics were a part of this architectural race by referring to the lack of support for Studio Libeskind on the grounds that the practice is from Germany - a country that was not supporting the Iraq War. It is, of course, impossible to measure accurately the impact of world politics at large on decision-making. As much as it is difficult to prove whether the media has influenced a decision such as the selection of the World Trade Center site competition winner to go one way or another, competition juries tend to want to be seen to be above being influenced by third parties. Yet Garvin writes, 'On February 27, at an internationally televised press conference Governor Pataki and Mayor Bloomberg announced that they had decided to proceed with the Libeskind scheme – a scheme which was acceptable to the players whose approval was necessary for anything to go forward. Its poetic evocations of the "Freedom Tower" set against the Statue of Liberty, "Wedge of Light", and exposed slurry wall that emerged from the innovative design process resonated with the public.'

If the public's opinion was a decisive factor for the decision-makers to select a winner, surely, the means of communicating the proposals – primarily the media – were, ultimately, vital to the equation. This is in addition to the other components that Garvin cites: '... parcelisation and street pattern, traffic flow, marketability, constructability, development cost, phasing, memorial setting and', last but perhaps not least, 'public reaction to each scheme'.

Federation Square, Melbourne

Melanie Crick

Lab architecture studio was thrust into the media spotlight in 1997. It had won the international competition to design Melbourne's Federation Square – Australia's largest cultural and urban project since Sydney's Opera House. At the time of winning this prestigious competition, it was a small London-based practice that was committed to providing an architectural laboratory devoted to learning, teaching and designing. Its philosophy, methodology and approach to architectural problem-solving were highly developed but not yet tested. Up until that point none of its projects had been realised.

Federation Square threw Lab into a welcome arena where all of its ideas would not only be built but also scrutinised by all sectors of the community. However, the project also put it into an unfamiliar level of practice that was not one of pure architectural mechanics, but a minefield of political and media wrangling. In short, Lab, through necessity and in very swift time, became wise to the power of the architectural image and its conduit: the media.

Like many publicly funded buildings, Federation Square suffered an exacerbated process fuelled by changes to government, objecting community groups, changes to the brief and budgetary crises. The protracted battle for Federation Square to be built was almost a facsimile of the political hoopla surrounding Australia's other famous landmark, the Opera House, a comparison that does not make the indigenous architectural community proud.

Lab, who had been transplanted from London to Melbourne, was faced with garnering support for the AU$450 million [approx £180 million] project. The site, an entire urban block in downtown Melbourne, was to be transformed from a railyard into a cultural and civic precinct which would provide Melbourne with an 'iconic' heart. The community and the media were excited. It was generally felt that the city, and this very strategic site, was deserving of new and insightful architecture. Support grew and the project gathered its own domestic and international media momentum.

However, at a critical time for the project, there was a change of state government. Federation Square was already partly built when it was decided by the incoming government, who like most opposing political parties had an acrimonious relationship with the previous commissioning government, that a crucial component to the scheme was to be 'modified'.

The architectural implications of this decision were severe. The 'shards', as the buildings in question were known, were located on the principal corner entry into the site. In design terms they were anchoring devices that simultaneously introduced the scheme to the city and invited the city into the public plaza. Their location also framed a historical vista to St Paul's Cathedral and this proved to be the basis for the directive to 'alter' the scheme.

Initially, there had been opposition from the National Trust and the Anglican Church in regard to Federation Square's relationship with the cathedral. Whilst these groups expressed their overall support for the design they were concerned about the 'shards' and sought for them to be changed. Lab consulted with these groups and agreed amendments were made. However, the Church and the Trust still held reservations but that might have been that had it not been for the change in government.

A full government review of the project was

**Lab, Federation Square,
Melbourne, 2002**

Previous page
The proposed 'shards' had
a respectful relationship
with St Paul's Cathedral.
They were to accommodate
a visitor information centre,
hospitality suites, an exhibition
centre and offices. They were
connected by an underground
passageway

This spread
The 'shards' were to make
a definitive entry into the
public plaza. They effectively
completed the 'square' and
enclosed the public plaza

CITYSEARCH.CAFE

ordered and the result was an instruction to dramatically reduce the height of the tall slender 'shards'. The architects were not consulted during this review and despite their pleas, were not privy to its contents until the Premier publicly released it. The other financial partners in the scheme – Melbourne City Council and the federal government – were in support of retaining the buildings as Lab had proposed them but had no sway over the commissioned report.

Lab had no choice but to appeal to the public via the mouthpiece of the media. All private appeals to the Victoria state government for a mediatory solution were ignored and the unusual steps of fostering support from the architectural community and civic groups in the mainstream media were adopted. A frenzy of letters, opinions and headlines (both supportive and in opposition to the design) were published beside bespoke renderings of the buildings

in question. The project was no longer being promoted by the state government and the site was shrouded in a hoarding, not allowing the community any visual access to the drama that was unfolding.

The media played the key communicative role during this period. The newspapers became the forum for the battle. Lab appointed a media consultant to assist it and learnt the process for this type of defence as it was being played out. It stood firm in its belief that the removal of these architectural elements would diminish the sensibility of the entire project and voiced this expert opinion strenuously.

The battle, however, was lost. The directive to reduce the height of the west shard from six storeys to two was implemented and Lab was left with a very disappointing architectural scenario. It had fought for its vision through the most powerful means available to it but, like Utzon in the 1960s, was unable to make its voice heard loud enough.

Project Case Study

Birds Portchmouth Russum Dorma Door Handles, London

Will Jones

Image is an important part of any business concern in the 21st century, from the typeface for a company logo to the perception of a prime minister. Architect Birds Portchmouth Russum (BPR) is a small London-based practice with a limited portfolio of built work. However, it is perceived throughout the architectural world as a practice that creates radical, sometimes extreme design solutions.

This is not the easiest way to become commercially successful but it does attract the attention of the media, especially when these designs are backed up by exquisite architectural drawings that would not be out of place in an art gallery. The practice needs only to release a drawing for a design competition and it will be pounced upon by a mob of design press.

It is this marketability that has allowed BPR to move into different areas of design including engineering, product design and exhibitions. One such venture was the design of a range of door handles for manufacturer Dorma.

The door furniture manufacturer, although massively successful as a low cost bulk supplier of product, wanted to lift its profile and be recognised as a design conscious innovator within its field. Dave Bradshaw, former Dorma sales executive, explains: 'The appeal of breaking this part of the market comes from the fact that if specifiers want your door handle, the visible bit, then they will almost automatically purchase the rest of the door furniture – hinges, lock and keep, door closer and kick plate – from you, too. That is what Dorma was aiming for'.

Dorma approached BPR. 'They wanted a boundary breaking design', says partner Richard Portchmouth. 'Like the new Selfridges in Birmingham, they wanted

to reinvigorate a known brand'. The practice duly designed a range of handles the likes of which had never been seen before.

Almost before the designs were off the drawing board, the manufacturer and architect were being inundated with enquiries about these strange new door handles. Architectural and product design press ran entire spreads devoted to BPR's designs, something unheard of even when star architects and designers like Norman Foster or David Chipperfield venture into the product design marketplace.

The initial wave of publicity in publications like *World Architecture* and *Architects' Journal* was immediately followed up with the unveiling of the product prototypes at London design exhibition Spectrum. This was no ordinary unveiling. BPR designed and built a luxurious stand of sleek black doors, each sporting one of the new door handles. On opening each door, the visitor was treated to a cubicle clad in studded red leather, completely mirrored or glaringly white. At the centre of each rear wall was a model, design sketch or image of Dorma's company history.

'The practice, brought in to raise Dorma's design profile, has succeeded beyond its wildest dreams', screamed *Architects' Journal* in September 2002. 'The whole effect is a surreal mixture; a cross between a 19th century brothel and a crazy house at the funfair'.

Visitors to the stand were entranced, flitting from one door to the next, excited at what they might find behind each. 'It was a massively successful stand,' says Portchmouth. 'People loved the designs and the way in which they were presented. They would even fetch friends on to the stand to see the spectacle.'

Is It All About Image?

Previous page
Birds Portchmouth
Russum for Dorma UK,
Dorma Door Handles, 2000
Radical door handle design
makes for successful
marketing and the exploration
of new possibilities in an
otherwise rather uniform
industry

Left and opposite
Birds Portchmouth Russum,
Plashet School Footbridge,
London, 2000
Where engineering meets
architecture; the Plashet
School Footbridge creates
a radical sculptural
intervention between
two school buildings over
a busy road in London

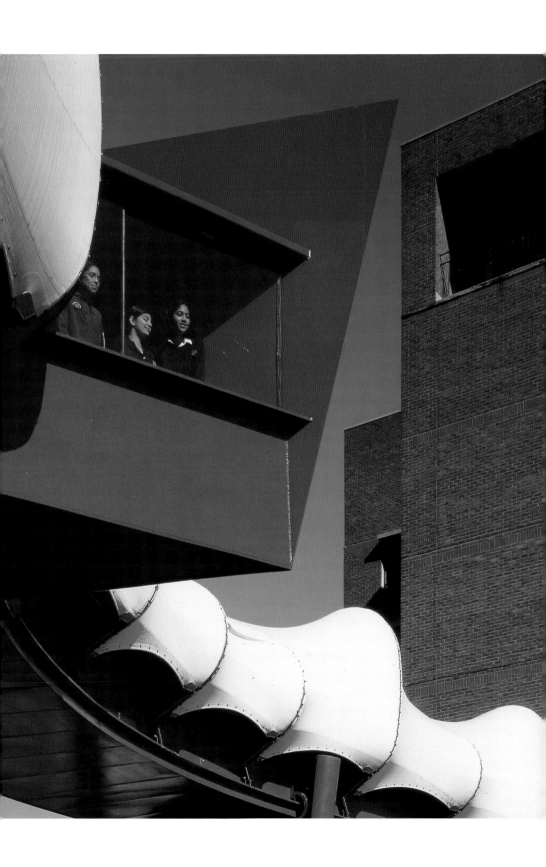

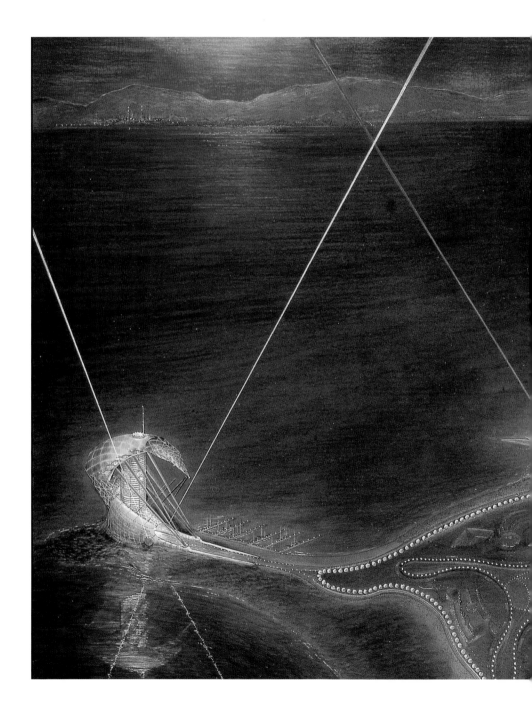

Is It All About Image?

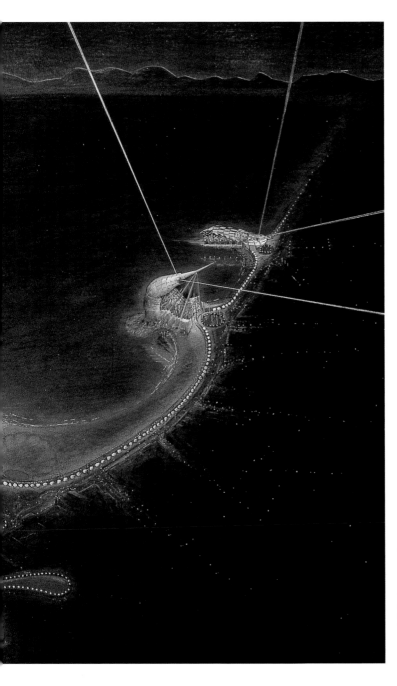

**Birds Portchmouth Russum,
Morecambe Seafront, 1991**
Exquisite drawings are an
integral part of how BPR
operates. This concept sketch
shows a giant shrimp-like
structure housing tourist-
friendly outlets and attractions.
It is part of a larger
regeneration scheme for
Morecambe seafront

Bradshaw explains: 'The stand worked wonders. People were coming up to me and exclaiming, "this is Dorma! We never knew you could do this, it's fantastic".'

The handle designs and the way in which they were first presented to the public had been a major success. It put Dorma on the map in the high design marketplace. This new interest in BPR and Dorma spurred the unlikely duo on. The stand was rebuilt firstly at London's most widely known design exhibition, 100% Design, and it again drew the crowds and a flood of orders for the handles. The high-end design press, newspapers and consumer titles including *Frame*, *Architectural Review*, and *Wallpaper** now picked up on Dorma's emergence into premium design sector. *Frame* (Issue 16) exclaimed: 'The stand was a totally unexpected container for Dorma's corporate identity. BPR has created a mini-museum, a curator's dream. With its secret compartments, the stand is a box of tricks, a spatially intriguing idea that calls for exploration.'

The practice was subsequently invited to display its body of works, including the Dorma stand at the Architekturmuseum in Basel Switzerland, an accolade afforded to star architects the likes of Frank Gehry, Herzog & De Meuron and Rem Koolhaas before. The partners even gave lectures entitled 'The poetic and the prosaic' in Basel.

'Dorma saw the potential in this European venture', says Portchmouth. 'It sponsored the exhibition. They could see the possibility of rolling out what was originally perceived as a UK brand internationally'.

This exhibition in Switzerland, speaking engagements and coverage in a plethora of printed press, in addition to the furore that the exhibition stand created, are proof that combining forces with a PR-friendly practice can be very powerful. The architect got the deserved recognition for a range of otherworldly designs that have not been matched to this day and the manufacturer hauled itself out of the low-cost volume supply market and into the design-led set.

Is It All About Image?

Opposite
Exhibition stand for Dorma,
Spectrum, London, 2000
Exhibition stand at Spectrum,
London 2000, for the launch
of Dorma's new door handle
range. A strong black presence
opens up into a 'box of tricks';
each new handle opens a door
onto a different aspect of
Dorma's design history

Below
Birds Portchmouth Russum,
Prefabricated Living Module,
nicknamed 'The Pacemaker',
1993
BPR explores innovative new
ways of rapidly creating a
home. This prefabricated living
module contains bathroom,
kitchen, utility space and all
services. It is simply
transported to site and 'bolted'
on to an existing living space,
making it ideal for barn or
warehouse renovation projects

Project Case Study
The Dutch Scene in Architecture

David Littlefield

Dutch architects appear to have some sort of cachet, a specialness. Government money helps, allowing practices to engage in expensive image-making exercises, but there is also something else, an 'x-factor' at work that gives Dutch architects a positive image simply by virtue of their being Dutch. This chapter explores how this public relations gift has arisen, and how architects have managed to sustain it.

Architectural audiences around the world sit up and take notice when a Dutch architect walks into the room. Importantly, this respect goes deeper than simple national stereotyping of the sort that associates Germany with quality engineering. The image suggests more than the fact that these architects are good at what they do; instead, there is some sort of assumption that contemporary, witty and thoughtful design comes naturally to these people.

Fanny Smelik, public relations manager at landscape practice West 8, says the advantages of this perception even filter down to relatively unknown practices, who use their nationality as a conduit for international publication. 'I think we do have an advantage ... I've worked in other offices which are far less famous in terms of people and design, but they've really benefited from having their work published everywhere'.

This is partly due to government help. The cultural missions of Dutch embassies actively push design as a distinctly Dutch talent, while subsidies amounting to at least 20 million euros have been distributed annually since 1988 at federal level alone. This has allowed architects to pursue research projects, exhibit their work and publish bold manifestos. MVRDV is a good example of a practice with a reputation as both a publisher of challenging research material and the

creator of exciting buildings.

Even international magazines buy into these marketing and public relations exercises. If they're not publishing special Dutch editions (like *Abitare*'s May 2002 edition or the RIBA *Journal* in May 2003), they're devoting entire issues to a single practice (MVRDV in *El Croquis* in 1997) or feting Dutch architects as guest editors (Lars Spuybroek edited the January 2000 issue of *Domus*). In fact, it is not uncommon for Dutch culture magazines to receive a public subsidy. Interiors title *Frame* was once rescued by a government hand-out worth £50,000 when it threatened to go bust. 'Thanks to that subsidy we could survive', says editor Robert Thiemann. Also, architecture title *Archis* gets an annual grant.

These tactics tap into Dutch architects' pride in the theoretical underpinning of their work. Moreover, that government support provides them with the confidence to give voice to their ideas in the absence of an actual building commission. 'The Dutch don't make things so much as they trade value, and thus have a strong focus on the manipulation of abstract information', says Aaron Betsky, director of the Netherlands Architecture Institute, who was putting together a new work, 'False Flat: Why Dutch Design Matters' as this book went to press.

This observation is supported by a set of phenomena that have coalesced to form what could be described as a national brand. Firstly, it is important to understand that Holland as a country is a designed product, its artificial landscapes being the result of a collective political, engineering and architectural will; three quarters of the Dutch built environment dates from the latter half of the 20th century. Dutch architects are just as adept at

Previous page
Mecanoo, Main Library,
Delft University of Technology,
Delft, 1997
Founded in 1984, Mecanoo
has had several principal
line-ups, including Erick van
Egeraat who has gone on
to make a considerable name
for himself outside the
practice. The firm, like many
of the more successful Dutch
practices, has managed to

maintain an international and
academic outlook through
prestigious teaching positions.
Partner Francine Houben has
taught as a visiting lecturer at
the universities of Philadelphia
and Calgary, as well as the
highly regarded Berlage
Institute in Amsterdam.
Similarly, Henk Döll has
taught at the Berlage Institute
and the University of
Technology in Vienna

Opposite
Office for Metropolitan
Architecture, Educatorium,
University of Utrecht,
Utrecht, 1997
Rem Koolhaas, via academia
and his practice OMA, has
become the iconic figure
of contemporary Dutch
architecture. As well as
teaching at a long list of
prestigious institutions
including Harvard, Koolhaas

has a knack of
compiling his work
in eye-catching
publications like
S, M, L, XL (1995).
This building for
the University of
Utrecht, an exercise
in spatial fluidity, is one
of OMA's more important
works and is often
seen as an influence
in student projects

masterplanning as they are at designing individual buildings. 'The whole country is architecture, as 70 percent of the central part is reclaimed land, and thus an artificial construct', says Aaron Betsky.

Secondly, the Dutch tradition of providing exemplary social housing, which goes back at least a century, has led to a particular strength in this field and has provided young architects with plenty of work. Until recently, it was not unusual in Holland for architects under 30 to have a clutch of built works under their belts.

The result is a two-way process whereby architects contribute to a national culture for design which in turn provides those architects with a status that professionals in other countries can only envy.

Evidence of this respect is not hard to find. In July 2003, the Royal Institute of British Architects, for the first time in its history, took its annual conference beyond the shores of the UK – to Rotterdam. In October of the same year a RIBA judging panel, set up to assess student work for its prestigious President's Medals, comprised British architect David Adjaye, Kasuyo Sejima from Japan, and two Dutchmen – Ben van Berkel and Wiel Arets. In May 2002 the entire edition of Italian design magazine *Abitare* was a 'Speciale Olanda' (Holland Special). The magazine did the same thing in 1985.

Abitare's leader in its May 2002 issue is instructive: 'The sheer amount of new building and the variety of [Dutch] technical solutions, coupled with lively manifesto-type engagement and radical theorising about the not-too-distant future, form a corpus and climate of experiment which at the present moment is virtually unparalleled in the rest of Europe ... Ever more vital and pluralistic, Dutch architecture impresses foreign observers with its pragmatism and love of experiment that make the country seem a paradise for architects.'

It is the experimental side of architectural life that stands the best chance of securing government funding. Landscape practice West 8, for example, is in receipt of 75 percent of the costs of a new billboard project which will enliven the journeys of Dutch motorway drivers from summer 2004. These inflatable structures, containing key messages for those passing by, would not have been possible without public help.

Unfortunately, this extended honeymoon period may be grinding to a halt, requiring architects to think more carefully about the way they create and project their image. Crucially, good PR is accumulated gradually, and must be nurtured constantly. Henk van der Veen, director of the student award body ArchiPrix, is now not so sure the Dutch reputation is fully deserved. The subtle and hard to pin down PR machine which has elevated the nation's architects to such high international regard should be reined in, he believes. Indeed, Dutch confidence is in danger of becoming arrogance, he says: 'Maybe [our architects] are regarded too high. There should be more of an international discussion, but they're shouting too loud. There's not a two-way conversation'.

Moreover, although he remains convinced about the quality of the best student work, van der Veen says the fact that architecture courses are not as long as they used to be is causing a decline in the quality of 'average' students. This is causing practices to become lazy, where they will mimic the work of strong practices without bothering to engage in, or publish, research of their own. 'There's no critical reflection of what they're doing ... MVRDV's proponents among other bureaux think "We can do that". But that should not be the case, and it's wearing a bit thin', says van der Veen, critical that good detailing is being sacrificed to gimmicks.

Indeed, Bart Lootsma, author of the book *SuperDutch* published in 2000, has come to the same conclusion. Although the book would not have been possible without financial help from the Netherlands Architecture Fund, a careful reading of the text shows that it is the product of a very independent and critical mind. Lootsma has suffered a little from the perception that the book is a government-sponsored piece of marketing material, which it is not. He also makes no secret of the fact that even the title (suggested by his British publisher) was perhaps a mistake. It greatly annoyed Rem Koolhaas, who considered it arrogant and nationalistic. The more successful Dutch architects, believes Lootsma, prefer to market themselves as international characters. 'No one wants to be SuperDutch any more – not even myself', admits Lootsma, who now lives in Austria and is convinced that the quality of Dutch architecture is slipping.

Is It All About Image?

Is It All About Image?

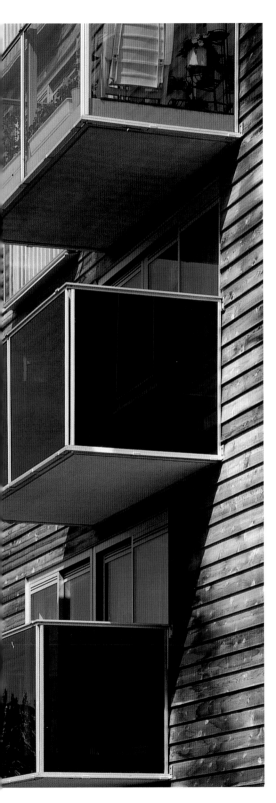

Opposite
MVRDV, WoZoCo housing development, Amsterdam, 1997
This housing development (whose odd name derives from the Dutch 'Woon Zorg Complex', which translates into English as the more prosaic 'sheltered housing development') is among MVRDV's early works. The 100 units are aimed at people over the age of 55, but the practice's response was a distinctive and cheeky statement – in terms of both architecture and image-making. The projections from the building overcame tight masterplanning constraints

Below
West 8, Borneo-Sporenburg houses, Amsterdam, 1994-2000
The private houses in Borneo-Sporenburg, Amsterdam, are representative of the new contemporary style housing with which the Dutch are now so strongly associated – colourful, fresh and often high-density. The masterplan for the area was conceived by West 8 Architects who wanted to provide a variety of housing types as opposed to uniform housing developments. A number of individual architects were commissioned to realise the housing designs, which aroused media interest in the notion of a new way of living

Is It All About Image?

Left, top and bottom
West 8, Schouwburgplein, Rotterdam, 1996
West 8 has arguably put landscape architecture back on the Dutch design agenda. In this scheme the practice has reinvented the idea of the public square by raising it slightly above the surrounding area, creating a stage, and altering the materials according to how the sun strikes the space. The more shaded west side of the square contains a poured apoxy resin floor incorporating leaves of silver; the sunnier eastern side is marked by a bench along its entire length and consists of warmer materials such as timber and rubber. Four hydraulic lighting elements, reminiscent of the local port's cranes, can be altered interactively by the inhabitants of the city. The square is a huge success with the public by giving itself over to different uses at varying times of day – sitting, skating, strolling and even football matches

Below right
West 8, Schiphol Airport, Amsterdam, 1994–8
West 8 takes the position that landscape architecture should not be presented as a counterpoint to the city. It is, instead, about creating inhabitable spaces that blur the distinction between the two. The landscaping project at Schiphol Airport provided the perfect site for an exploration of these ideas, as well as an opportunity to present the practice's work to the widest possible public. While offering crisp, artificial landscapes, West 8 also adds traditional Dutch elements such as tulips

This page
SuperDutch

SuperDutch was published by Thames and Hudson Ltd in 2000. Written by Bart Lootsma and designed by Mevis en van Deursen, it is interesting how very early on the phenomenon of the active promotion of a 'Dutch approach' to architecture was recognised within the country. In this media-savvy society, it is hard not to get a critical response to any band-wagon approach. As much as groups and cliques are required to get ideas established, they are very quickly surpassed

Is It All About Image?

This page
West 8, Horizon Project,
Randstad, 2003–4

In West 8's Horizon Project, sponsored by the government as a public art project, the practice designed a set of large billboards to be sited alongside the motorway system. Using images of cows as a metaphor for both happiness and loneliness, the practice poses this question: 'The cow is the co-existent consolation in our hectic existence. The eternal cow in the eternal emptiness. Apparently these obvious values cannot exist on their own. Is it true that these values could only exist as a cliché on a postcard in a souvenir shop, on the package of milk or on a billboard across the road?'

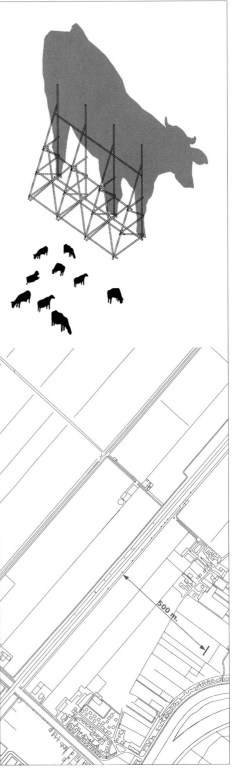

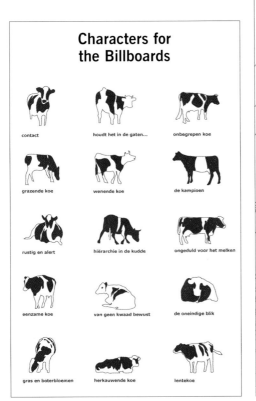

Characters for the Billboards

contact

houdt het in de gaten...

onbegrepen koe

grazende koe

wenende koe

de kampioen

rustig en alert

hiërarchie in de kudde

ongeduld voor het melken

eenzame koe

van geen kwaad bewust

de oneindige blik

gras en boterbloemen

herkauwende koe

lentekoe

Portrayal

What the Media Say

Press

Picture Editors

Publishing

Print

Politics

Purpose

Is It All About Image?

Public Relations is very much about second-guessing what the media want to hear. The better we understand what different types of journalists want from us, the better our chances to target the publications with the right type of approach and material. In this chapter, I have interviewed eight different architectural writers to find out how they view their potential subject matter in terms of PR, architects and the buildings they design.

The architectural writer on a national newspaper will have a different readership and agenda to a writer in a glossy design magazine or trade journal. Often, on a newspaper, the architecture or design contributor is fighting for space with other arts correspondents. It is not just the architect pitching to the architectural correspondent, for example, but the correspondent then taking the idea to their arts editor.

It helps if the architect or their PR has prepared the pitch in a way that is ready to be taken that step further by thinking, 'How is my project relevant to the average person reading this column or slot? Does it represent new government policies for better healthcare facilities, prove that an award-winning, architect-designed house can be done on a modest budget, or show the potential for design excellence using prefabricated building methods?'

The wider an audience one is trying to reach via the media, the more important it is to think of the other cultural phenomena a building might represent. Of course, style is another matter and many of the lifestyle supplements in the newspapers prove that one can access wide audiences by supplying stunning photographs of private houses, in particular, but bars, cafés, restaurants and hotels can get good mileage, too, if they are fashionable.

The glossy monthly design and interiors journals work very much on the basis of a graphic interpretation or critique of whether something is suitable for the page.

The look of this type of publication is important to the publisher and even if a building is of real merit, it just may not fit in with the overall style of the magazine. This type of graphic consistency can apply to the advertising as well.

Editors do change the way a publication will do things. The better you know what makes an editor or writer tick, the more chances to appeal to their areas of interest. A new editor may decide to have a broader, less image-driven approach to selecting material for publication than their predecessor. Or the contrary.

Some editors are keen on exclusives, others are not that bothered. This is often to do with individual temperaments, although most would argue that it is do with competition between publications. More likely, it is based on the level of journalistic instinct. Some editors and writers get a buzz from breaking a story, while others are happy to contribute to a debate from a new or original slant.

Architects are often too busy thinking about things from their own perspective to tap into ways to engage the press. If wholly focused on what one's project represents to one's practice, one may miss out on, for example, learning about why a journalist might be interested in actually publishing the project. For instance, an architectural correspondent or freelance writer might be an opera or theatre buff or sit on a committee for the protection of historic monuments and thus have a vested interest in writing about a subject that combines their interest in buildings with their other pet topics. It is also good to get to know which writers steer clear of what. If someone can't stomach Minimalism, it may be unwise to try and solicit their attention with the latest white-walled extravaganza with its Zen garden. It may lead to coverage but may well also backfire.

When pitching to the media, architects often wonder if there is some pre-existing agenda that determines who gets published. They may ask, 'How important is the reputation of a practice for you when considering a publication?' The case studies of the journalists interviewed here shed light on this question. The interviewed writers also explain what, for them, makes up the identity of a practice. This is important when considering how someone from the outside world actually formulates a working picture of a practice, something that enables this person to categorise the architect as potential source material for particular subject areas.

To get an image across to the outside world, a practice is left to certain devices like visuals and the web. To help the reader understand what the media would like to see when receiving such information, I have asked the journalists interviewed here: 'What kinds of images are most useful to see? What do you want to see on a website if you use these?' The answers reveal that the workability and ease of assimilation of the core aspects of information are key.

Architects often say the only reason they bother with the press is to get more work. The journalists' comments about the relationship between the media and how it influences potential commissions tell of how difficult it is to pin down cause and effect in this equation.

When commissioning a PR agency, or having someone proactively promote a practice on your behalf, it is important to know that what is being done is not counter-productive or, worse, damaging to future relations with the media. To gauge what kind of promotional activity is welcomed and what is actually a nuisance, the interviewed journalists were asked: 'What kind of promotional activity for buildings is constructive or obstructive in your view? What helps? What is actually superfluous?' From the responses we had to this question, it is clear that those pushing projects for publication are not always attuned to how best to succeed.

Finally, to address the topic of the book, is it all about image? The notion of whether architecture is currently too image driven is discussed with this group of journalists. There are polar opposite views on the subject, which only reiterates that in PR there are no safe and fast rules that apply from one case to another. PR is really about learning to tailor one's approach. At it's best, it is a very bespoke service which treats not only clients but members of the press in as nuanced a way as possible.

'Journalism loves to hate PR. It has become the norm in the media to knock us, whether for spinning, controlling access, approving copy, or protecting clients at the expense of the truth.'

'Well today's PR is the journalist's black book. And, of course, the PR machine responds to the realpolitik of the media marketplace -

feeding the unstoppable, insatiable appetite for stories or exclusives that provide a competitive edge.'

'Journalists need PR not just to give information, but to provide access to sexy spokes-people to fill columns, host programmes and give soundbites.'

WHY JOURNALISM NEEDS PR
Extracts from an article by Julia Hobsbawm in
The Guardian Monday 17 November 2003
© Julia Hobsbawm

The Guardian, UK
Jonathan Glancey

David Littlefield & Laura Iloniemi

The Guardian offices
The Guardian was founded in Manchester in 1821. It is Britain's only independently owned daily broadsheet paper. Now located in Farringdon Road, London, the paper has recently opened a News Room visitors facility that allows access to its archive. This is indicative of the culture of openness of *The Guardian*. Uniquely, readers have free access, without the ordeal of registering on-line, to the paper's web-site. Stories are posted on the very day that they appear. Columnists are allocated individual websites. For Jonathan Glancey see: www.guardian.co.uk/glancey

The Guardian is one of the UK's leading broadsheet newspapers, with a largely liberal, left-of-centre readership. Published six times a week, this newspaper has a circulation of around 386,000, the vast majority of which is UK-based. Its weekly architectural report appears every Monday in G2, the newspaper's supplement covering general features and the arts.

Jonathan Glancey, *The Guardian*'s architecture and design editor, says that national newspapers can exert a great deal of influence over the development of architecture and the sort of buildings that get commissioned. The trouble is that newspapers often fall into the trap of reporting practices that already have a strong media presence. This can have the undesirable effect of strong reinforcing prejudices.

'As with any subject or discipline from film, stage, music, sport, the national media tends to have casts of characters who dominate its pages. The more prominence they are given, even when undeserving, the more their position is reinforced by those with the power to commission buildings', he says.

Is It All About Image?

'Media coverage needs to extend to practices other than those that naturally attract headlines. A good many architects are overlooked by the media because they do not produce sensational work, nor do they mix in media circles. It is not particularly easy for critics to find space for more obscure practices'.

On the other hand, it tends to be the editors, rather than individual critics, who are most persuaded by the strength of a practice's reputation. However, even critics feel they must play the 'celebrity game' to some extent. 'New talent must be sneaked in', says Glancey.

Glancey also warns practices and, by extension, their PR teams to be very careful in their attempts to garner the support of critics. Too often, PR companies spend considerable time, effort and money on trips, events and elaborate media packs – much of which is unnecessary. 'Some journalists love trips, others avoid them like the plague. Some love "dos", others don't,' he says. 'PRS need, as best they can, to tailor their approach to the needs and style of particular writers and publications.'

Having said that, it is fair to say that all journalists want good, clear information. Funky exercises in graphic design are generally off-putting, even obstructive. 'Glossy brochures on pink paper with texts in trendy typefaces go straight in the bin – especially those abounding in architectural cliché'.

The same is true of websites: 'These need to include clear imagery, clear facts and no gobbledegook writing'.

Where PR teams can really help is in putting the writer in touch with the architect and arranging site visits. A press release should arouse the interest of a writer but should never be considered a substitute for an actual conversation or a first-hand tour of the building. Otherwise, journalists are left with the unenviable task of writing about a building in the abstract. 'That is never a good idea', says Glancey.

Financial Times, UK
Edwin Heathcote

David Littlefield & Laura Iloniemi

Financial Times
Edwin Heathcote, architectural correspondent of the *Financial Times* says that, 'The architectural press is obsessed with exclusives. The national press is not. They each assume their own readership will not have read the competition. This is how it should be, editors should have the confidence to review what is best and not worry about who else has written what.'

The *Financial Times* (FT) is an international, UK-based business newspaper with a circulation of 434,000, six times a week. The vast majority of copies are bought outside the UK – 288,000 copies are sold around the world. Importantly, the FT is not just a business newspaper; its general news reporting, selective coverage of the arts and its international outlook make the FT a highly regarded, quality product.

Edwin Heathcote, the FT's architectural correspondent, warns that good PR does not guarantee media coverage. What matters is the strength, integrity and persuasiveness of a practice's ideas: 'There is no substitute for thoughtful, well-designed buildings. No matter how much you spend on PR', he says. 'The identity of a practice should be based on substantial design work, either realised or unrealised. But this isn't always the case. Of course, any practice's work can be enhanced by presentation or successful networking, but these can only supplement good work.'

Heathcote is a firm believer in the fact that good architecture is difficult and that the most powerful buildings are not necessarily the most photogenic. This presents a problem because he also says that good photography is crucial to attracting the attention of critics and getting one's work published. Images do need to present the building in context, therefore architects need to refrain from showing the completed work as an isolated object. He also stresses the importance of a good sketch: 'Sketches (not CAD) can be very useful in helping a journalist begin to understand a style or an approach. Intelligent text – not PR blurb – is also critical'.

Heathcote worries that too much architectural image-making is based on the 'one-liner' – a dramatic, eye-catching, easy to understand visual that looks powerful but is intellectually shallow. Heathcote blames much of this on architectural competitions, which depend on judges quickly ploughing their way through large numbers of entries.

'Images of a blob, a skeleton, a frame are easier to explain and to illustrate. But they are one-liners, with no depth there can be no real longevity unless the idea is absolutely brilliant. The competitions system encourages this kind of one-liner as judges need to understand the building in a flash. This is a significant problem', says Heathcote.

The trick for architects is to be able to convey thoughtful design in a manner that is graphically engaging – something that can be summed up succinctly without running the risk of losing the ideological depth of the scheme.

'Architecture is always going to be image driven because it is easier to build that way. The most profound buildings are often not photogenic; often, they are all about space, light, material, transition and narrative. They are about being there', Heathcote says, adding that taking the time to illustrate a clever idea, rather than resorting to a quick one hit wonder makes long-term business sense. 'It is easier to build up a portfolio of striking images than of slow, thoughtful buildings. But the latter is what will keep you in demand.'

Heathcote adds that a practice's website can go a long way to explaining the philosophy of its architecture. Even simple elements like the number and nature of the links on the site can be very suggestive of the interests, passions and inspirations of a practice: 'You can tell a lot by what links are on a site. It can be a sly way of intimating what your interests are.'

Architectural Record, USA
Robert Ivy
David Littlefield & Laura Iloniemi

Robert Ivy
Robert Ivy, FAIA, is an architect, writer, and editor. Since becoming Editor in Chief of *Architectural Record*, the magazine has grown to become the world's largest professional architectural publication, encompassing both print and the internet. Under his leadership, AR received publishing's highest honour in 2003, the National Magazine Award for General Excellence. A frequent spokesperson for the profession, he travels extensively for the magazine and has broadened its coverage to include more international projects. In 2003, Ivy was named Vice President and Editorial Director of McGraw-Hill Construction Publications

Architectural Record is one of the most prestigious USA architecture titles. Published monthly, this well-resourced and well-staffed magazine has a circulation of 113,000 (11,000 of which are outside the USA), which is extremely large for a magazine of this type. This New York-based publication not only carries well-written, and well-photographed, building studies, but news and thoughtful feature articles. Special supplements on interiors and residential projects are published quarterly. The AR also runs an excellent website: www.archrecord.construction.com

Robert Ivy, editor of *Architectural Record*, says publications like his have a 'profound' influence on the course of architecture, both as a source of technical data for practitioners and as a marketplace for potential clients. Apart from that, professional magazines act as a sort of benchmark, providing architects with yardsticks against which they can measure and position themselves.

He says, 'Magazines serve not only as sources of information covering news, and pragmatic matters, but also as scanners of the architectural field. Magazines publish models of creative and compelling work for the international community and thereby give architects projects to emulate, to react against and to reflect upon in contemporary discourse.'

To actually make an appearance in these titles, Ivy offers a handful of simple tips: provide hard-copy images and well-written information; make available the exact addresses of completed projects (allowing writers to scout out potential stories privately); and don't for a moment think that persistence will culminate in publication (it won't). 'Press kits, press tours, meeting the architects, and good professional photography all help any given project. Press releases and aggressive marketing are superfluous.'

Ivy says that he prefers architects to supply hard-copy images because the ease with which electronic pictures can be sent means that numbers become unmanageable: 'For *Architectural Record*, hard copy is the best format for us. We collaborate at editorial meetings and pass around material. It is too time consuming to print out the immense volume of electronic images that we receive for these kinds of meetings.'

In spite of many criticisms to the contrary, Ivy denies that architecture is becoming too image-driven. Yet image-making (and the power of the single architectural image) is important, he says, to encourage greater debate about the subject and raise the level of exposure that architecture has in the public eye. Useful discussion can easily coalesce around strong images. 'Architecture is not too image-driven. However, we do need more interaction between architects, their projects and the public. Image-driven architecture can get more information out there and allow for more analysis and criticism in the media and the pubic sector', says Ivy, adding that issues such as housing and post-occupancy evaluations have a tendency to be ignored: 'These do not get enough attention'.

Ivy also observes that many practices have recently embarked upon a process of deliberate branding. 'Identity is a self-conscious decision for architects nowadays. Many architects discuss and debate the identity of their practices – whether they achieve the desired identity is another story. For example, sometimes architects want to be considered "hands on" or "craft-oriented" or "collaborative" or "gender specific". This wasn't the case in the past and only in certain cases is this identity construction important or helpful. Sometimes it can be confusing or misleading.'

Indesign, AUS
Paul McGillick
David Littlefield & Laura Iloniemi

Cover of *Indesign*
As far as the character of a practice is concerned, Editor Paul McGillick says "this is a complex thing. Obviously, it is heavily dependent on the principal(s). But given that most practices don't always choose the projects they get to work on, their approach becomes crucial. In broad terms, this is about whether they start from the outside-in, or the inside-out and the relative weighting of issues like function, meaning and art versus habitation."

Quarterly Australian magazine *Indesign* is only a couple of years old but has already established a good reputation as a source of intelligent writing. Concentrating on architecture and interiors, *Indesign* pitches itself at commercial and 'top end' private consumers.

Editor Paul McGillick argues that architects and interior designers need to take PR seriously if they want to broaden their appeal and client-base. Publishing represents an important channel of communication between the design profession and potential clients, especially if practices want to present themselves as accessible and non-elitist.

'I think there is a continuing need to demystify the profession and make it more approachable. This would be in the profession's interests, as it means a broadening of the market of potential clients. Hence, promotional activity which makes architecture accessible is valuable – likewise anything which emphasises affordability and the fact that it is not as hard or as expensive as many people think to obtain a personalised design. This implies, by the way, a willingness on the part of the profession to collaborate with clients, rather than dictate to them,' says McGillick. 'Highly academic architectural publishing is clearly superfluous to all but a small number of people. At the end of the day buildings are about everyday life and should be presented as such.'

Like many other journalists interviewed for this book, McGillick wrestles with the issue of whether or not the reputation of a practice should affect decisions concerning publication. Like most, he stresses that individual projects should be judged on their own merits, but he concedes that he can be influenced by the mere fact of reputation. Importantly, though, McGillick has set out to spot less well-known designers, or even those who (for one reason or another) actively steer clear of publicity: 'For me the reputation of the practice is not of great concern. Of course, there is some cachet in publishing the work of leading architects, and that is certainly a part of my thinking. On the other hand, I think perceptions distort reality considerably, whether it be in architecture, literature, music or whatever. Certainly in architecture there is a lot of fine work done which is ignored by the architectural press, either because it does not conform to prevailing ideology or because the architects can't, or won't, play the game of promoting themselves. Many architects are shy or, sometimes, suspicious of going down that path. An important part of my editorial strategy is to unearth quality/left-of-field projects so that the magazine exposes the full range of design and not just a narrow part of it.'

Part of McGillick's strategy is also to explain buildings as habitable spaces rather than as pieces of sculpture. Although he calls photographs 'misleading' because they inevitably misrepresent the actual experience of a building, he admits they are 'essential' for publication. However, he is also keen to reproduce detailed drawings and concept sketches in an attempt to convey the process of design.

McGillick argues that architecture is too image-driven, but adds that the whole of contemporary society is 'ocular-centric'. Although there is architectural criticism which emphasises the actual experience of a building and its appeal to all the senses, rather than just sight, McGillick worries that there is too much emphasis on buildings as sculpture and too little focus on how they work for the people living and working in them. 'This is changing, even in the area of commercial interiors. But there is still a hard core of architects and architectural teachers who abstract architecture', he says.

Interestingly, McGillick tends to ignore websites as being 'too restricted'. Rather than browse a website, McGillick will ask for a set of digital images to be emailed to give him a 'preliminary' look at a project.

Abitare, IT
Daniela Mecozzi

David Littlefield & Laura Iloniemi

Cover of the 40th Anniversary Issue of *Abitare*, October 2003
The editorial reads, regarding *Abitare*'s past, 'It has evaded the battleships of the information society with the speed and manoeuvrability of a corvette, enjoying a degree of curiosity denied of other less agile publications.' It is very true that *Abitare* has succeeded in its founder, Piera Peroni's remit to see beyond fleeting trends and never limit itself to houses or homes, nor creating a magazine by architects for architects. Moreover, *Abitare* has had a relatively unchanged staff over 40 years

Abitare is a monthly, Milan-based title published in both Italian and English, with a circulation of over 60,000. Covering architecture, design, interiors and the arts for 40 years now, this well-presented, glossy magazine contains intelligent building studies and does not shy away from making political statements. International in outlook, *Abitare* draws on correspondents from around the world, largely based in Europe, the US, Australia and Japan.

Daniela Mecozzi is *Abitare*'s UK correspondent. Although she believes that the reputation of an architectural practice is an important asset when pitching for work, Mecozzi warns that publishers take a different view – journalists prefer to let a project stand on its own merits and are careful not to let reputation interfere with editorial independence: 'As a journalist, the reputation of a practice is a relatively unimportant element; it will not lead to the automatic selection of a project for publication. Projects are fundamentally considered and selected by publications on the basis of their own merit.'

Once you have a project of publishable quality, Mecozzi says that attracting the attentions of journalists depends on two crucial factors: clear information and decent images. Information loaded with hyperbole, or which quickly glosses over the subject matter, is superfluous or even obstructive. Importantly, text should put a project firmly into its context and include details of the brief, an explanation of the architect's response and views from the end user. Some of these elements are often ignored by architects in the presentation of material, especially explanations of the geographical and social context and the impact on users – an outline of these factors would definitely grab Mecozzi's attention. Crucially, the best kind of promotional activity is, says Mecozzi, 'one that provides clear information'.

Apart from that, architects need to be able to guarantee access not only to themselves, but to the building and its client; there is little point in trying to conjure up publicity for a building commissioned by a media-shy client who will block visits from inquisitive critics.

Good images are also very important to getting published – in particular, those which 'capture the overall sense and sensibilities of a project'. Mecozzi believes that architecture is currently too image-driven, but pictures which sensitively explain a scheme would go a long way to countering this criticism. Computer-generated images are the worst offenders, even if they are often seductive and striking. 'Some computer-generated images have little to do with the real project, and are actually more interesting than the project itself', she says.

Websites can also be useful and effective publicity tools, especially those which successfully provide an understanding of the identity of a practice, the combination of people and ideas, and how those ideas are translated into a body of work. Importantly, though, websites should be simple to navigate and, again, Mecozzi would like to see project explanations which include non-architectural voices: 'I want to see clear, simple and fast to access sites. I want to be able to get an all-round perspective of the projects including, where appropriate, the views of the clients and the end-users.'

Mecozzi warns, however, that achieving publication is no guarantee of winning further work. Some clients are more susceptible to publicity than others while, equally, some keep a keener eye on the professional press. Publication can lead to a greater public understanding of a practice's approach but, importantly, it also encourages debate and raises the level of architectural awareness generally.

'As a means to making projects more widely understood, and commissioned, publication affects certain clients. The reality is that the number of such clients is still limited,' says Mecozzi. 'I think that writing about architecture encourages debate within the profession and it is at its best when it encourages debate outside of the profession.'

Architectural Writer, UK
Kenneth Powell

David Littlefield & Laura Iloniemi

New Architecture in Britain
Written by Kenneth Powell, published by Merrell and launched in October 2003, it is a sequel to Kenneth Powell's publication *New London Architecture* (Merrell, hardback 2001; paperback 2003). Such books are important in placing architects within their generation and the milieu they are working in at a given time. They provide an opportunity for less established firms of architects to be published alongside the best-known practices, and for their work to be considered as part of a cohesive debate on the future of building

Kenneth Powell is an architectural writer who contributes to a wide range of journals and book publishers. He is also the author of a number of weighty monographs, including books on the Richard Rogers Partnership and Alsop Architects. He has written several books that provide overviews on recent British architecture, most recently *New London Architecture*.

Kenneth Powell has mixed views about the way in which architectural writing influences the course of the profession and the way buildings are commissioned. Like most media figures, he concedes that publicity is generally a good thing and that media attention can go a long way towards forging an identity for the practice – but, he warns, publicity often only tells half the story.

'There is a sensational element in things which are written about purely as fashion. Good work can be perceived as dull. Writing creates a reputation for practices, a basis for placing their work which does influence short-listing. People who have a good public image and PR get the jobs,' says Powell.

'You get very ample coverage of particular buildings, like the Disney Hall or the V&A Spiral, or on issues like tall buildings. These are spectacular things that will always generate public interest. Things like Will Alsop's proposal for Liverpool's Fourth Grace even made it into the news pages, rather than just the arts supplements. But this does give the impression that architecture is a series of spectacular events, rather like fireworks. Of course, that is only half of what architects do ... the problem is that people might think this has very little relevance to them. Having said that, some of the property supplements, which used to be very commercially focused, show a real understanding of design issues.'

Powell says the best way to create a positive practice image and generate media attention is simple: 'Do good buildings, or at least buildings which generate discussion'. A good example of this, he says, is Hampden Gurney School by BDP, which was short-listed for the 2002 Stirling Prize – although BDP is a highly successful practice, its media profile was very low until then.

This building is also an interesting example of architecture as a visually commanding profession as well as a potential answer to social problems. As other contributors to this book argue, buildings with a strong social and cultural agenda give journalists another reason to write about them. 'We all want to write about architecture as an art, which encourages interest in form, but we must emphasise social qualities. Regeneration and urbanism need to be discussed more than image. Reviewing should be more open; no-one assumes that a play or opera is reviewed once only.'

Having designed something good, Powell says attracting media interest is best done by putting together clear information sheets which promise access to the architects and, where appropriate, the client. PR puffery and glossy brochures are, he says, simply a waste of time: 'A lot of rather spontaneous stuff arrives, some of which is very dull and will never get coverage. Everyone on a press list gets critical and ruthless; it's easy to chuck away material'.

Moreover, Powell adds, information sheets can also be a useful resource for a practice – too often, he says, the corporate memory is lost when staff leave or projects simply recede into the past. Well-designed data sheets can serve as useful prompts when projects are gathered together for something like a monograph.

As for websites, Powell says he 'hardly ever' looks at them. The problem is that too few sites are properly resourced and too many are difficult to navigate. He reserves praise for the Foster site, however, which he says is an exemplar of what an architectural website should do: allow the user to quickly source information. The best sites, he says, are those which act as databases, allowing users to compile lists of projects by, for example, completion date or building type. 'Fosters do it very well and it's certainly one of the best. It basically does the job of getting you the information.'

Robert Thieman and Billy Nolan

David Littlefield & Laura Iloniemi

Dutch bi-monthly *Frame* is an English-language magazine that is available worldwide (circulation 24,500). Concentrating on cutting edge, idiosyncratic interiors and installations, *Frame* features the work of large international practices as well as small and relatively unknown outfits. Beautifully designed and well-illustrated, *Frame* is also interested in the relationship between design and contemporary art practices.

Like other contributors to this book, *Frame*'s editor-in-chief Robert Thiemann and editor Billy Nolan have an ambivalent attitude to the question of whether an architect's reputation can or should influence a magazine's decision to feature a particular project. Predictably, they insist that the quality of the design should be the deciding factor, but they also point out that big names provide a marketing opportunity for magazines themselves. In fact, they go further – if magazines and newspapers play a crucial role in establishing an architect's reputation, they argue, why shouldn't they share a little of the glory?

This also provides a spin-off benefit for lesser-known practices. A big-name feature might act as a hook for potential readers, and as a Trojan Horse for small firms to present themselves to the public. Appearing in the same issue as a star architect might be no bad thing.

'In principle, reputations are not essential. Originality and quality of design are paramount', insist Thiemann and Nolan. 'Nonetheless, it is important to feature recognised figures every now and then. They owe

Frame Cover

The November–December 2003 issue of *Frame* magazine makes one think of how doors are opened for young architects through publication. *Frame* was set up only seven years ago in Holland. The contributors are based internationally, writing in English about what is happening in different parts of the world from Scandinavia to France and the United States. *Frame* has been a significant forum for a large number of young practices to get their work published and an important magazine in pushing new media and thinking about design in general, rather than just buildings

THE INTERNATIONAL MAGAZINE OF INTERIOR ARCHITECTURE AND DESIGN > NOV/DEC 2003

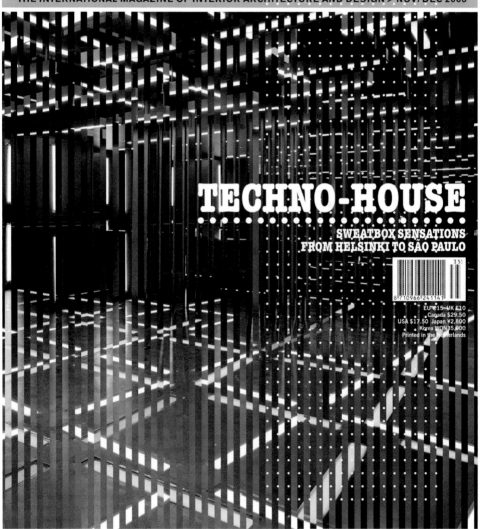

TECHNO-HOUSE

SWEATBOX SENSATIONS
FROM HELSINKI TO SÃO PAULO

EU €15 UK £10
Canada $29.50
USA $17.50 Japan ¥2,800
Korea WON35,000
Printed in the Netherlands

their fame to the media and we from the media can, in turn, profit from their fame. Big names offer the reader a foothold for what the magazine is about.'

Thiemann and Nolan also admit that the massed ranks of the media can be unpredictable and that there is often little sense in who gets published and who doesn't. They are certain, though, that aiming for publicity is an important aspiration for any practice, largely because it makes good business sense. Yet, they argue that the degree to which architectural writing actually affects the direction of the profession is less clear: 'The true influence of writing on the profession will only become clear in the far distant future. However, architectural news travels fast in the global village. It doesn't matter where we live or even what we read, we all have access to the same information. Some projects and practices are published everywhere, whereas other projects and practices feature nowhere. There's no logic behind the mechanism of the media, but it surely influences the profession in that it has a large bearing on how and to whom projects are commissioned.'

Interestingly, Thiemann and Nolan consider that media coverage is also an important factor in shaping the identity of a practice. Beyond the individuals who work there and the list of completed projects, identity is something to which the media contribute. Consequently, practices should think very carefully about whom they pitch projects at, editors with whom to establish close relationships, and even when to seek publicity: 'The identity of a practice is shaped by its designs, its realised work and its media profile – how often they are featured in the media, in which media, and in which way.'

When seeking publication, Thiemann and Nolan insist that architects submit images which, 'expose the intention behind a design as clearly as possible', rather than pictures limited to straightforward visual appeal. Having said that, they are sanguine about the fact that architecture is an image-driven industry. That has always been the case, they say: 'Architecture has always been image-driven. On the other hand, every aspect of the building profession has its own niche publication: we have magazines about details, architectural history, construction, housing, building economics and so forth. Every aspect of building gets its fair share of media attention.'

Lastly, Thiemann and Nolan offer a guide to the ideal website – easy to navigate, providing an overview of the office's range of work, with lots of pictures and explanatory texts. 'What's more, it should contain all relevant contact details. Anything else is superfluous.'

Frame **Stand** designed
by Dumoffice for the 100%
Design Fair in Rotterdam,
2003. Design and
architecture magazines are
often represented at various
international trade fairs.
The editor's presence at these
types of events has been
important for the editorial
team of the publication to
forge links with architects and
designers around the world

Robert Thiemann & Billy Nolan
recipe for maximum media coverage

Spend some time working for an architectural heavyweight with the right media image

Set up on your own and make sure everyone knows where you've worked

Try your luck in competitions and make sure you produce the most seducing (read: unbuildable) renderings. Publication is only days away

As soon as you get a commission to actually construct something, issue a press release accompanied by even more seductive renderings backed by a hint of an architectural theory (see Step 1 for inspiration)

Repeat Step 4 again and again replacing renderings by actual construction photos as work proceeds

As soon as construction is finished, hire the most published architecture photographer, invite a busload of well-known media people, and get that buzz going

You're famous now

To remain so, keep fine-tuning Steps 4 to 6

Monument, AUS
Fleur Watson

David Littlefield & Laura Iloniemi

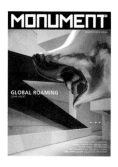

Cover of *Monument* Magazine
The editor of *Monument*, Fleur Watson says that, 'There are clear divisions in architectural publishing in Australia between the academic, professional and public pursuits. At *Monument*, we attempt to bridge the professional and the popular by providing a context where ideas are able to be communicated to a wider audience without "dumbing" down the content or alienating the reader with architectural jargon. *Monument*'s extremely high image quality and large format is a deliberate attempt to engage the wider community to be involved with the process of architecture. Architects also appreciate seeing their work in this context as it gives them a vehicle in which to engage their clients – we've had several reports of an article leading to a new commission for a project.'

Monument is a well-respected Australian architecture and design magazine. Published six times a year, this outward looking title will put non-Australian projects on its cover as proof of its international credentials. Staffed by a small number of people, *Monument* relies heavily on its extensive network of international editors - the magazine has representatives based all over the world covering cities as diverse as Los Angeles, London, Paris and Tokyo.

Editor Fleur Watson has a mixed view of the way conscious image-making can benefit both individual design practices and the architecture profession generally. Her concern is that public relations can be 'formulaic' and that architecture is in danger of becoming too image-driven; buildings that are designed to look good on a magazine cover, regardless of the quality of their spaces, do not represent good PR in the long run.

However, Watson also believes that specialist publications like *Monument* are important tools in the creation of an architectural community. 'I'm not sure that publishing architecture influences the process of producing architecture; I believe that architects will do what they do best regardless of what critics or academics might have to say about a project. However, I do think publishing has an important role in creating a sense of "community", both within the architecture profession and among a wider readership, to facilitate an important forum for sharing work and discussing ideas.'

Importantly, Watson places a stronger emphasis on the quality of work rather than the reputation of the architect when considering schemes for publication. Yet there is a problem when it comes to 'celebrity' architects who often define the image of their practice. Celebrity, she says, often has little to do with the quality, but is a useful PR tool in raising public awareness of architects and their work. Reputation versus design integrity often puts magazine editors in a quandry – unless, of course, both are present.

'I'm more interested in the work rather than that of an individual practice. However, particular practices do offer a calibre of work that is known to be exemplary through a commitment to, and investment in, design research. Beyond this, if the editorial team receives an outstanding submission from an unknown practice, of course we will be interested in reviewing and publishing,' says Watson.

'Individuals who lead a practice usually define its identity, but identity may also be created by an iconic project, a competition or built work. The concept of an architect's emerging personality and celebrity is certainly a new phenomenon in the general media. I'm not sure that the architect-as-celebrity has any relevance to the quality of work produced, but perhaps the attention given to the individual is useful in raising awareness of what architecture can and does contribute to our culture.'

In Australia, at least, a sure way of receiving media attention is taking on a publicly funded project. Any large public building receiving government funding is sure to be a constant source of debate in Australia's general media. Melbourne's Federation Square, undertaken by British practice Lab architecture studio, in association with local firm Bates Smart, is a good example. This daring scheme was accompanied by a 'media frenzy' which created both positive promotion and negative obstruction throughout the life of the project. Nonetheless, in spite of what Watson calls 'endless dialogue' on both political and architectural matters (which forced some alteration of the finished design), the building has become a success: 'The public has embraced this building and is using the spaces as they were intended to be engaged with.'

F is for Foreword, a genre of the publishing world promoted within increasingly ubiquitous monographs. Intended to lend gravitas to what are essentially examples of vanity publishing (see V), they are intimately associated with the name Kenneth Frampton.

T is for Timing. Publishers (like editors) love an anniversary, a new building opening, an exhibition. Any excuse to give a book a certain (usually bogus) topicality – or as a newspaper an excuse to roll out a big general article. Don't expect any type of media to be interested in waiting to publish a building till it's actually finished. That'll be too late – anyone could have seen it.

V is for Vanity publishing. The deal works like this: practice wants a showpiece of its work, or sometimes all of its work. Publisher sets up a deal. Architect does all the picture and drawing research, spends endless hours with author, corrects proofs – and pays the publisher for the privilege...

'An Alphabetical Guide' by Paul Finch, extracted from
This Is Not Architecture edited by Kester Rattenbury, Routledge (2002)
pp 199 and 202

Portrayal
Laura Iloniemi

Photography

Editors want to see good images. Some are even willing to alter these to make the magazines look good. Architects, too, have been known to take out lampposts from streets, and the like, to give the perfect picture. Architectural photography is loaded with a desire to control and represent buildings in a certain way. The photographer's task to deliver this to his client is not an easy one.

It feels almost a platitude to say that visual fields, like architecture, depend very heavily on imagery to tell their stories. This is true even when the topic is perhaps not that image-driven. For example, architects can generate very interesting studies, research or masterplans that are really text-based idea stories. Yet, to get these published, it often pays to produce an interesting image.

Photographs, even if only suggestive of their subject matter (e.g. a site or aerial shot), are useful because, unlike drawings or computer renderings of publishable quality, they take less time for design teams to produce. However, photographs can be pricey if done by a professional or they require a lot of setting up. Yet, their power in getting a practice seen, and without much other PR assistance, tends to be worth the investment. In fact, if a practice does no other PR, the best thing it can do is set aside a budget for a portfolio of excellent photographs of its work.

Editors tend to warm to good photos even if they may know that the building in real life is not that exceptional or even resolved as a piece of architecture. After all, editors are under pressure to make their magazines look good. How many times does one visit a building that, impressive on the pages of a publication, was a disappointment in reality. The American Museum of Folk Art in New York by Tod Williams and Billie Tsien is a good example of such a project. It won the World Architecture Award in 2002 and hit the pages of architectural journals internationally. As is, sadly, too often the case neither all the members of a panel judging buildings nor all the journalists writing these up actually go and see them. Instead, far too many 'assessors' and 'critics' depend heavily on photographs. It is true that this is a curious state of affairs because any critical reflection on architecture should depend on a spatial and contextual experience of buildings. However, the reality of what drives the media is, for the most part, skin-deep and the savvy practitioners consider this in their approach to publicity by flaunting what lies on the surface.

Buildings can change quite dramatically and, unfortunately, many recent buildings, in particular high-tech ones, have altered for the worse while in use. This is why photographs are often the only record of a project as intended by the architect. They are an ideal means to put forward what architects consider important about their work and express the design quality that architects would like their future clients to buy into upon commissioning a potential job. Thus, photographs are a real marketing tool, not only in the media, but in pitching for new business.

Renzo Piano Building Workshop, Aurora Place, Sydney. Photographed in January 2001

Previous page
The photograph of the Renzo Piano designed office building subtly indicates its place in Sydney by showing a bit of the Opera House in the foreground. Shots such as these are popular in the press as they give a sense of place to a project and highlight the importance of its location with a major city centre or near a well-known monument

Below
Architects often mention wanting to have people in photographs of their buildings. Yet, this happens very rarely or in a very discrete manner. Long exposures that make the occupants of a building ghost-like are increasingly popular as they do not detract too much from the architecture.

Generally, there is a strong desire to control the environment so that it appears like a perfect composition, more like an artwork than a place to be. This compulsion to capture the 'ideal' conditions is understandable as it is the only moment that the architect appears to have full control of how a completed project is perceived in real life

Is It All About Image?

Yet, the types of photos required for publication can differ from what is suitable for practice brochures or documents specifically targeted at commissioning bodies.

Some architects like to have two or more sets of photographs for different purposes. For example, a few architects have recently used fairly abstract black and white photography to highlight the poetic qualities of their work for the purposes of illustrating thematic texts and essays on the practice's œuvre. For magazine publication, the same practices commission full colour photos done in a classic architectural photography style that focuses on the compositional qualities of the designs. A choice of photography, be it in different styles or a sheer number of varied views of a building, is useful if one is looking to maximise coverage on a project because magazines prefer not to publish the same images as their competitors.

Photographers are noticing how practices are welcoming the idea of having people in their photos to better demonstrate to clients, in particular, how their buildings are used. Populated photographs are good in terms of providing imagery that comes across in an accessible way. Yet, photographers will be the first to say that it is a real skill to make people look natural and sit comfortably in a building. Having an awkward figure in a shot can ruin its potential for publication. A stylish shot using models, like dancers, can actually enhance coverage for a project that without this type of photographic styling may not get as far with editors. A safe measure that does not require hiring models is to use long exposures in which people appear as though they are moving and fade fashionably into the image. This is appropriate as people or other elements of styling should never be the subject matter but the background of architectural photography.

The surroundings of buildings can also be useful for maximising the publicity potential of a project. Architectural photographers will know that even a modest building shot against a major landmark will fare better in terms of getting picked up by the media. International journals, in particular, enjoy receiving photographs that attach a project to a known plaza, cathedral or other monument, thus making its geographical location immediately apparent. A New York yellow cab or a London double-decker bus are also the types of urban clichés that help to locate images well.

Architects can fret over the weather conditions under which they are paying for a shoot of their buildings. Too many think that only a sunny

Henning Larsens Tegnestue,
Nordea Bank, Copenhagen.
Photographed in May 2002

This spread, overleaf &
pp 172–3
Peter Cook says that,'Buildings
can be summed up, for the
most part, in four to five
pictures including details,
overviews, shots concentrating
on material and spatial
qualities, sense of presence,
context.'

summer day will do. Some buildings can benefit from a bit of frost, trees with leaves changing colour and casting deep autumnal shadows, or even melancholic mist and light rain. Again, the poetic effects of weather can help dress a building in a way that assists in media potential. It should be borne in mind that some magazines will be unreceptive to publishing very seasonal shots, like ones with snow in them, in other than appropriate months. This is true of lifestyle oriented magazines, although these publications often commission their own photography, as do newspapers.

As an architect, one should consider carefully which photographer to choose, especially if one wants to get away with only a single set

of shots per project. What is the image that one would like to get across and what type of photographer is best suited to achieve this? Buildings can be captured in a very artistic way, as was often done in the 1930s by great photographers like Lucien Hervé who has recorded Le Corbusier's work. Hervé's photos master the abstract qualities of a building, framed views, the play of shadow and light, sculptural forms and textures. Very few photographers have this approach to buildings today.

A number of photographers are taking reportage style images of buildings which work very well where a sense of the building's dynamic as a part of the city is concerned or when the buildings are occupied. There is also, of course, the whole realm of lifestyle magazine photography in which beds are left beautifully unmade, designer beauty products are carefully placed in bathrooms, or other such tasteful items are left in view as though by accident.

Perhaps the most prevalent approach to architectural photography is the sequence of architectural shots which captures the internal and external spaces and elevations in a thorough manner, working from general shots to detailed ones. Predominantly, this means a set of shots that does not include people and is achieved just after completion of a building and prior to its occupation. Such shots are sometimes criticised for being sterile or not being about the very fact that buildings are made to be used.

In *This Is Not Architecture*, Jonathan Hill writes, 'The architectural photograph has a number of roles, one of which is to present the building as a higher form of cultural production to defend and promote architects and patrons. Many architectural photographs display similar characteristics, such as perfect climate and no people, because they mimic the perfect but sterile conditions of the artwork in the gallery.'

Yet, the popularity of this type of photography amongst architects surely reveals something profound about how practitioners experience and want to envision their work. One should not be ashamed of just admiring pure line, form, shape, contrast of light and shade and all the wonderful stuff of building. Perhaps one of the most influential architectural photographers of our time, Julius Shulman, set a precedent for this Modernist vision.

Interview with Architectural Photographer Peter Cook

London-based architectural photographer Peter Cook has been photographing buildings since the late 1970s. Like many architectural photographers, he sees some of the world's leading examples of contemporary design first hand and close up in every stage of build, time of day and season. Few architects or magazine editors have this type of breadth or hands on experience of buildings. To follow is a short interview with Peter Cook.

What makes a good architectural photographer?
Perhaps the best way is to train as an architect as the technical side is relatively easy. You need to understand the building. I am inspired by drawings and elevations.

What is the best way for a practice to brief an architectural photographer?
Architects sometimes give you a set of digital printouts of what they want you to technically do. This is not a good way. If I wanted you to do a house, I wouldn't photocopy pictures of houses of how I want an architect to put it together. The best brief allows for seeing in a different way and accepting that this is what happens when you commission a photographer. Architects should show photographers plans, drawings and not other photos as this bends your mind with a certain image in your head.

Architectural publicity is unlike other forms of PR. What is special about the architect and photographer rapport?
As architectural photographers, we are actually dealing with the architects' clients. Photographers who are arrogant can put clients off. One needs to reassure the architect's client that one is not disruptive but discrete.

Yes, a shoot that has not gone well can put an architect's client entirely off the potential of publicising a project in any way. Do you have the promotional value of a project in mind when you shoot?
Yes, I try and achieve a cover with upright shots, taking into consideration the graphics of a magazine we might be aiming for publication. In the Wilkinson Eyre Bridge shot, I had the idea

of getting a ballet dancer for the shot. I saw the graphic and knew that this shot would go down well. Also magazines ring you up and ask, what is going on? I like to suggest to them what the younger practices are up to.

What are the most common pitfalls or mistakes made when commissioning architectural photography?

Sometimes my clients want to see everything in a picture or make the building look big and impressive as part of pitching the practice's work to a client. A photo will never do that because it is a two-dimensional form. Shooting unfinished buildings is a common problem with hours of waiting and difficulties with scaffolding about.

Yes, magazines often drive the rush to get a building photographed, scooped before anyone else. When should buildings ideally be photographed?

Winter light and bare trees are good and sculptural; contrary to the obsession of waiting for spring and trees to be in leaf. The best light is in autumn and spring. This is to do with cloud formations. When the weather front goes through, the rain clears the atmosphere and you get deep blue skies and puffy clouds. High pressures of the summer months result in milky light that is not good for photography. Yet, there is a fixation about photographing buildings on sunny days, although sun is needed for providing side light for texture. Not overhead light, though, like you get in the summer. Best thing is to leave the photographer to decide on the quality of light. Photographing buildings, you have to know about meteorology.

Wilkinson Eyre, The Royal Ballet School Bridge, London, 2003
Peter Cook's photograph of the Royal Ballet School dancer was an instant hit in the architecture media. It was the photographer's idea to have this type of image taken in view of how it would bring the building to life and captivate readers. It is interesting to note that to achieve the image the Royal Ballet School had to be happy with how the dancer was posing in the photograph

Peter Cook lodges his photographs with a picture library called VIEW which is in regular contact with editors, picture researchers and art directors, thus providing a free PR service to the architects whose buildings are shot by VIEW photographers (for further details see: www.viewpictures.co.uk). Peter Cook does emphasise that it is important that the photographers liaise with the architects about who material is sent to, especially in view of client sensitivities and agreed rights of first publication with magazines. The great benefit of issuing material through a picture library is that only transparencies or high resolution scans that meet publications' standards are despatched to the media with the speed required for what are often very tight deadlines. There is also a computerised database that allows for tracking images for their return. This can be a great relief to a practice with limited resources to manage an image database.

Top 10 tips
for supplying
magazine
editors with
images

1   Never block someone's e-mail by sending huge, unsolicited image files (over 1MB)

2   Ensure CDS are clearly labelled and accompanied with colour printouts of their image contents

3   Ensure you know who owns the copyright of the images (it is usually the photographer) before sending out and whether there are fees to be paid to a third party like a publisher upon reproduction

4   Find out whether your photographer lodges images with a picture library and, if so, what might be the benefits or possible drawbacks

5   For important publications check what kind of material is required for best reproduction quality, e.g. drum scans or transparencies

6   When providing information digitally check how images and drawings should be saved for reproduction

7   Consider saving all digital information in three file sizes: high resolution for large scale or top quality reproduction; medium resolution for e-mailing for reproduction; low resolution for the web, viewing only purposes or Power Point

8   Create a naming system for all images that makes it easy to find and recognise them; consider ease of understanding these names at the recipient's end

9   Remember to keep records of image credits (photographers/ computer rendering companies etc.) and provide editors with this information

10 Keep a record of any material that has been sent out and a back-up so it can be easily reissued if lost

Portrayal
Laura Iloniemi

Presentation

The profile of a practice is made up of everything from what it produces on paper, and what is in the press, to how its offices look and how partners and other senior members of staff perform at interview. Additionally, the way meetings with media and potential clients are managed is key for the outside world to formulate an opinion about a practitioner. Presentation, in the widest sense, goes hand in hand with a practice's public persona or image.

Too often, architects resort to using the same information or presentation material to seduce clients and convince planners as they use for media purposes. The internationally renowned practices whose projects we might admire on the pages of architectural journals tend to know better. They will produce separate presentation material for the architectural press and, it is often said with some disdain, even draw concept sketches after the event, as it were, when their buildings have been completed. The better their images, the more these practices tend to get published. Very often, the press will say, great story, but do you have any good images? And a less great story will get in on the basis of 'just' a good image. In fact, it is not seldom that one sees a rather vacuous project getting wide coverage on the basis of being compelling to the press with eye-catching visuals.

The consumer media are largely attracted by similar presentation materials, as is the general public and the lay client. Such imagery tends to capture the mood of a project, while being exciting and easy to understand. Recently, computer renderings have become popular in achieving such goals as they are immediate in a similar way to a photograph. They make a project seem, perhaps, more achievable as they require little imagination to envision the outcome.

**Below
van Heyningen and Haward,
Birkin Haward landscape
for Gateway to White Cliffs,
Dover, 2001**
Birkin Haward believes in
exploring a site by sketching
it. The drawings for projects,
such as the one below for
the Gateway to White Cliffs
for the National Trust at Dover,
exemplify this approach.
They create a mood, a feeling
for a place that aids in
understanding what is required
from the new building
contextually. The drawings
thus very much demonstrate
a design sensibility

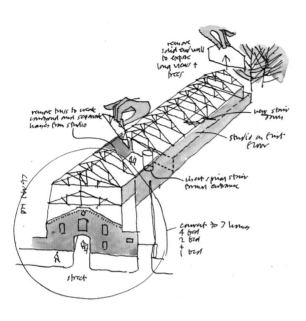

Left
van Heyningen and Haward's
studios are remarkably
comfortable to work in. As is
immediately clear from this
environmental diagram, this
is achieved through creating
a top-lit space with natural
ventilation, acoustic pin-
boards, appropriate lighting
and floor based services.
The drawing style opted for
here helps to explain how
the environmental strategy of
the building comes together.
The drawing sums up in a
single image how such design
facets can, by being present at
once, enhance the experience
of being in such a space

Bottom and opposite
Joanna van Heyningen and
Birkin Haward have created
a studio atmosphere in their
offices in London that is very
welcoming to both visitors and
staff. The original cab depot
building has been generously
converted by the architects so
that the building now consists
of some housing, two
courtyards, office space to-let
and the practice's own studio.
There is plenty of pin-up room
on the walls for drawings and
reference imagery for current
projects. This brings to life
the team's work and creates
an attractive display of what
is happening in the office. van
Heyningen and Haward also
have a kitchen-dining area
where meals are cooked for
staff and visitors can be
received at lunchtime

In some ways, computer renderings can dull the spirit of a project by making things too explicit or by rendering elements more equally pronounced within an environment than they would be when it is physically experienced. It is certainly true that, at the moment, a vast number of practices' works look all too 'samey' when judged by the computer renderings they release. It is as though the medium has not yet caught up with the artform it is seeking to interpret. From a practice's image perspective, this should be considered carefully when communicating what is important about the particular firm and distinguishing it from its competitors.

Painting a picture

Practices that pride their working methods as being like those of a design studio often value a more artistic approach to their presentation drawings. These vary from the method drawings of Birds Portchmouth Russum, which are some of the most exquisitely executed renderings around, to the freehand diagrammatic style of Birkin Haward, who made this a staple at Foster and Partners before setting up practice with Joanna van Heyningen. Both are very accessible approaches for the layperson to comprehend. Birkin Haward's method has the added benefit of allowing for explanatory captions or the creation of story-boards that show the

various stages of a project, or its environmental strategy, without having to resort to lengthy text.

Some practices have partners who are known as artists, such as Will Alsop or Steven Holl who produce compelling paintings and watercolours to illustrate their ideas. These are especially effective tools for clients to gauge the artistic make-up of the architect. So are loose concept sketches, which make an impact by virtue of being the first impression of an idea, 'a stroke of genius'. In addition to drawings, collages, relief panels, working models and presentation models are effective ways to portray how an architect works and what a project will be about.

Large model workshops with mock-ups done to scale often impress clients and press alike, creating a mood of a real workshop, a place of creativity like an artist's studio. Sadly, this hands-on feel is far too often lost in architects' offices which are looking more and more like the work spaces of advertising firms, or even solicitors and accountants. Computers and files take over to the extent that a client or journalist can be very disappointed at seeing only digitally generated information.

Some of the most successful press meetings that I have been to have been carried out with the partners of a practice who have taken the time to sit with a journalist, looking at hand drawn sketches, working models and material samples, and occasionally sketching to explain what they are saying. Some of the worst meetings have been ones at which nothing is shown and projects are talked about in abstract terms, or where images are only shown on brochure pages or weakly reproduced laser prints.

van Heyningen and Haward, The Royal Society for the Protection of Birds, Rainham Marshes, London, 2003
van Heyningen and Haward have set up a company called MGI Imaging that specialises in architectural renderings. The images here are of the practice's project for a visitor centre for the Royal Society for the Protection of Birds in London, won by van Heyningen and Haward in the autumn of 2003. The style of rendering is more attuned to traditional drawing and accentuates light and shade and materiality in the building in a way a lot of recent computer rendering companies have not been able to achieve. MGI Imaging thus provides the practice with the types of renderings that van Heyningen and Haward want, but other practices can also commission images through the company. See www.mgimaging.co.uk

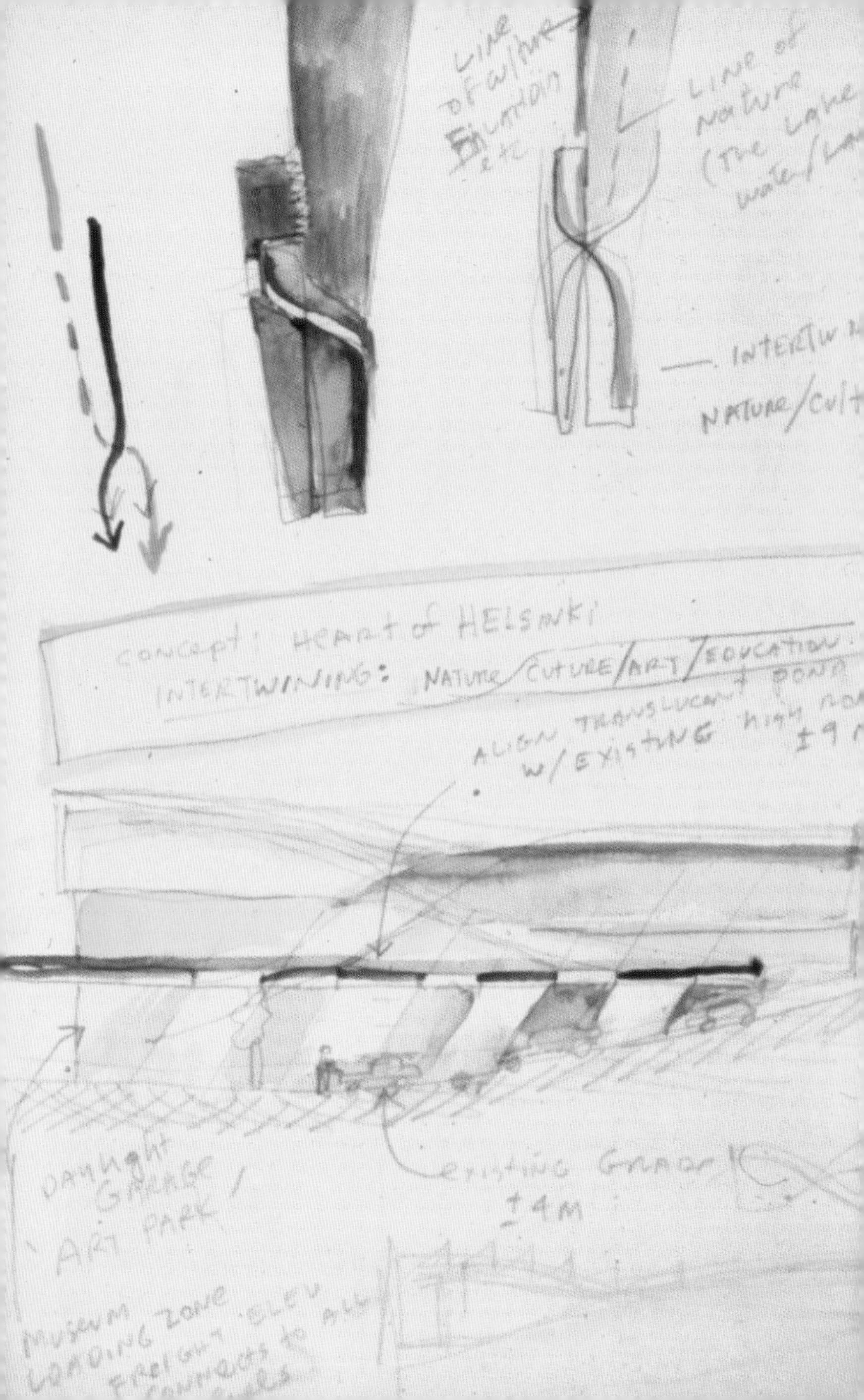

LINE of culture
EDUCATION etc

LINE of nature
(The Lake
water/La...

—— INTERTW...
NATURE/CULT...

CONCEPT: HEART of HELSINKI
INTERTWINING: NATURE/CULTURE/ART/EDUCATION...

ALIGN TRANSLUCENT + POND
w/ EXISTING HIGH ROA... ±9...

DAYLIGHT
GARAGE /
ART PARK

EXISTING GRADE
±4M

MUSEUM
LOADING ZONE
FREIGHT ELEV
CONNECTS TO ALL
...

It may seem fine to take one's practice brochure out if it contains the information required for an interview, but in reality it comes across as lazy. Making the effort to bring out original material or reference books containing material that inspired a scheme is a more attractive approach.

Architects should not be embarrassed by infusing their work environment and their visitors with an atmosphere of something a bit magical. Press interviews, in particular, can be a time to indulge in a bit of fun and to take stock of all the philosophical thinking that went into conceiving a project. It is not a time only to try and convince someone, like a client, that one is serious and competent.

Professionalism or Performance?

David Adjaye of Adjaye Associates once said to me that he finds it almost insulting to have to prove his professional qualifications. I couldn't agree more. Doctors, lawyers and other professionals are not asked, over and over again, to provide proof of their ability, or recent cases of similar experience. Yet, architects are constantly questioned, particularly in the UK, as though they were not providers of a professional service. This, in return, has had a rotten impact on how the architectural profession perceives itself, not only amongst the press but also when presenting to potential clients such as a jury panel.

Those with less chutzpah or innate charm end up doing the earnest thing of trying to convince the client that they are competent. Yet, the more established or highly thought of that the practices who are competing on a short-list are, the less they might worry about convincing their interviewer about quality assurance or the abilities of their consultants. Instead, these architects as individuals should really demonstrate how they could manage the project with their leadership skills, and their ability to work with the client and the authorities involved in getting a project through. The proposed design is key in winning over a client, but the best design may not pull through if the architect fails to be confident and convincing at interview.

A little showmanship is involved; yet, one should never try and become a presenter if this does not come naturally. Just like producing a drawing style that best communicates one's ideas, it is important to find the style that suits one in terms of appearing in front of an audience. It can be measured or quiet, casual or even a bit shy as long as one is able to take control of the situation. Audiences take to all sorts of personalities and

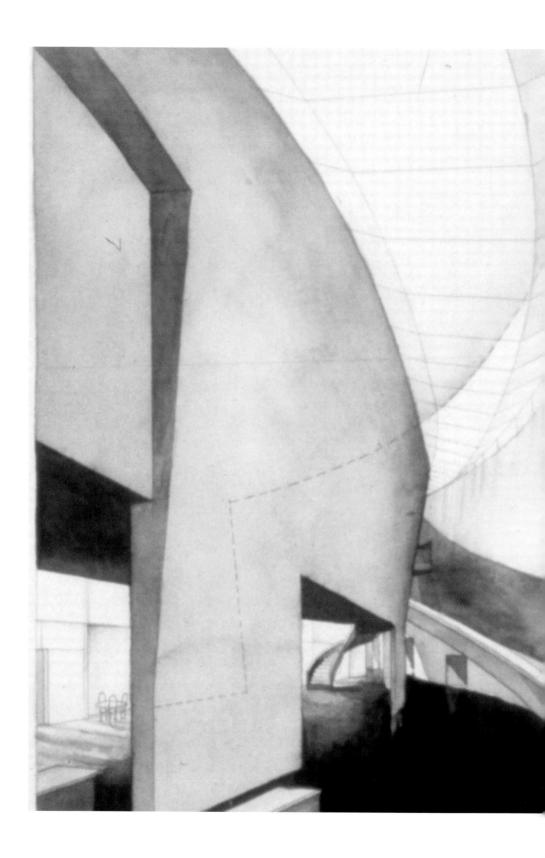

Left and p 190
**Steven Holl Architects,
Museum of Contemporary Art,
Helsinki, 1995**
The curators of the Museum of
Contemporary Art in Helsinki
(now called Kiasma) were
impressed by the quality of the
conceptual drawings produced
by Steven Holl. The sketches
and watercolour studies
represented the type
of artful interpretation that
the curators sought for the
building

**Above, right and opposite
Renzo Piano Building
Workshop, RPBW Studios,
Punta Nave, Genoa, 1989–91**
Located on top of a hill
overlooking the Genoese coast,
the Renzo Piano Building
Workshop Studios is amongst
the most memorable architects'
offices around. One not only
feels welcomed by a space
that honours its visitors and
staff, but there is a certain
pleasure in seeing an architect
surrounded by just the type of
studio setting that one might
use to stage a Hollywood
movie about a major designer.
Renzo Piano certainly lives up
to meeting any such
expectations

Is It All About Image?

can even find some odd behaviour charming, especially in creatives.

Architects tend to believe in what they do. In expressing it they should remember that sincerity and passion about what one does go a long way. Getting the audience enthusiastic about the things that one finds interesting or an asset in a proposed project is obviously a plus. At the same time, one must remember to take an interest in those listening, their concerns about a scheme or hopes of what it will do for their school, concert hall or hospital. One should always think, what can I answer, if the client comes out and asks, 'What do you know about us?'

PR may seem removed from what an architect chooses to do at their drawing board or how they pitch for a job. However, the imagery and the public profile of an architect are the very material a PR uses to promote a practice. What a bonus it is to have a client whose presentation materials help explain the design ethos of a practice or are so exceptional that magazines are eager to publish them. Who better to chair committees, speak at conferences, or be on radio or TV than someone who is a confident public speaker who has earned the respect of his peers by performing well at interviews and winning prestigious new projects.

The vast majority of architects would be too embarrassed to think of going to an image consultant in an effort to enhance their public profile. The question also arises whether such a consultant could, in fact, assist architects unless they know this highly nuanced world. Anyway, one need not go that far. In most cases, it is enough to not fight the seemingly unfair situation that success is not just about design, but occasionally involves a beauty pageant or a popularity contest. How one plays the game is a highly personal choice, but the more one enters into it in the spirit of a sport, the better the chances of winning. Similar rules apply to winning over the media. Present well and half the battle to become a sought after item is already won.

Interview with Rory Coonan

Rory Coonan, former Head of Architecture at the Arts Council of Great Britain and member of more than 20 architectural competition juries since 1996, provides some very interesting insights into what the judges of architectural competitions are looking for in their entrants.

What are the most important things to convey about one's practice when pitching for a job at interview?
It is important above all to convey hunger to do the job and not just to reinforce your view of your suitability to do it. Remember that you will generally have got as far as the interview only because it is already believed that you are in some sense suitable.

Therefore, it is better not to go over what may be old ground, such as the last few jobs you did, unless asked to do so. Instead, try making the generous – and flattering – assumption that the jury knows who you are and what you have done. This will leave you more scope and more time to develop a cogent case about why you have a burning need to do THIS job.

It is always surprising to me how many architects attend interviews out of an apparent feeling of duty rather than necessity. Perhaps they cannot bear not to be in contention with their peers. The higher up they are in the profession, the more this tendency – of diffidence, or lack of raw enthusiasm – is apparent. This attitude is always punished because juries do not like to feel that they have wasted a short-listed place.

In other words, an interview that is prospective, future-looking rather than retrospective – why your past makes you the right people – is generally more persuasive.

What about on paper; how should one come across when going for a job?
On paper, architects face considerable difficulties when trying to make an initial impression. This is because good graphic design is now universal. The opportunities to distinguish yourself from the pack are correspondingly fewer. Nor does content showing past projects always help: the narrow range of styles, the limitations of genre and the ubiquity of certain products within photographic representations of architecture, mean that everyone's brochure tends to look like everyone else's.

'Radical' approaches to presentation can work against your interest: the purpose is to be employable, not memorable: that can follow. Brevity is best. One option is to impress quickly by placing referees at the front – an impression of weight can be conveyed immediately by the quality and standing of the firm's supporters.

What are the most common mistakes architects make when presenting to a jury?

This is an easy one because I see them so frequently: the first is the common error of inviting people to be part of the team and then ignoring them. You would be surprised at how often people remain completely silent throughout an interview. This leaves the jury wondering why they were there at all. The impression created of incoherence in the team is likely to be indelible. At the very least, it sows doubts in jurors' minds. This is, of course, something to avoid. You would prefer any doubts the jury may have to centre on your design skills, not on your people management abilities.

A second common error is the minor discourtesy of rearranging the room, the furniture and generally seeking to make practical interview arrangements that differ from those by which other teams abide. The jury is likely to have planned these carefully. It generally resents upsets of this kind, which can create an unwelcome impression of 'special pleading'. For example, if you are requested not to bring electronic media – the booting-up of computers can waste valuable time – then do not do so, however much you think it may enhance your chances of success.

Another common error is not to stand up when speaking. Juries do not like bad manners. It also makes sense: by standing, you make yourself authoritative to a seated jury.

In your experience, what have been some of the best instances of architects overcoming, say, lack of experience through techniques of persuasion, conviction, or good presentation?

I challenge the premise of the question, which implies that lack of experience is a 'bad thing' that cunning arguments must overcome. But this is not so. In many competitions, the jury knows already what weight should be attached to experience, and is willing to make allowances for it. Generally, it knows too that mere persuasion seldom improves upon evidence.

Remember that the jury will contain members drawn from the client – that is, the users of the building – as well as from funding bodies. These people will be very concerned to judge how they can get on with you over several years. They are likely to be less interested to know how many times you have made the front cover of *Architects' Journal*. They will be sceptical of excessive claims and suspicious of attempts to project real experience through a cloud of expansive gestures.

A good presentation should never try to make a silk purse out of a sow's ear. It is better to lose honestly at the interview than to win a job for which experience later proves you to be wholly unsuited. Misleading claims you may have made at the interview concerning your competence will then be revealed starkly to all. This may set your career back a considerable distance.

What should a practice brochure tell you about a firm of architects?

Size, history, supporters, insurance, computing systems, quality assurance, successful projects (endorsed by others), ambitions, stability, annual turnover, bankers, membership of professional bodies and the brief, grammatically correct and properly spelled CV's of the principal players on the team for the job.

Avoid references to members' hobbies, family holiday habits, sporting achievements and the firm's charitable activities: while these may be intended to convey a warm glow of approval, they tend merely to embarrassment.

What do you think potential clients who organise a competition for a project want to achieve through this method of selection of an architect? What are their most common fears or aspirations?

Clients seek wider choice and better quality in the outcomes of their project. Their intention, initially at least, seldom has much to do with money: cheapness can be obtained by other means, far less arduous and less tortuous. The effort that goes into organising a design competition is such that no-one would undertake it lightly, so the aspirations behind it are likely to be 'high level' rather than merely to do with the pragmatics of how much space can be bought for a given sum.

Competitors stand a greater chance of success if they work out, from explicit or implicit sources (from the brief or from market intelligence) what these high level project ambitions are, beforehand. Experience shows that this approach reduces the odds of failure.

Clients fear having too few applications but this seldom arises in the United Kingdom, where scarcity of opportunity for architects fuels the competition system and helps drive up quality. This may sound harsh – the architect chasing many competitions and seldom succeeding – but it is not compulsory so to enter, merely voluntary. *Caveat emptor.*

Top 10 tips

for supplying magazine editors with information

1. Always include project name, location, function and a date of completion (anticipated if known)

2. It is good to supply basic information about the client and how the architect has responded to their brief

3. Architects should check with the client or their PR to see whether it is possible and when it is best to release information

4. It can be useful to provide more detailed information about the client as part of a project description; this can be in the form of a note to editors

5. Extra care should be taken in releasing often sensitive information about the cost of a project or, in the case of a private house, its location

6. All information should be up-to-date and have relevant contact details

7. Design team credits as well as those relating to consultants should be agreed before releasing to media

8. If copy on projects needs to be approved by the client, project architect or the partners, the approved version's text should be clearly filed

9. Image sheets of available press visuals are useful to post as hard copy or e-mail on a Pdf, but only if high resolution images are readily available on request

10. Ensure that the recipient is happy with the information. It is best to target the material to the type of publication, bearing in mind specific opportunities for news coverage and features

Conclusion

Laura Iloniemi

Presence
Pretence
Predominance
Pre-eminence
Pomposity
Power

Is it all about image? Well, images are certainly vital tools for publicity, as we have seen. They make a story by giving substance to even the insubstantial. Yet, this book says in a number of ways that some sort of identity – something that genuinely makes the practice or the architect stand out in the eyes of the public, be it through their design contributions or their persona – is certainly as important as images. This can range from the more subtle to the overt, although the more pronounced the identity the easier it is to get noticed. That said, if the identity is managed well, subtler messages are heard, too. Identity is formed by everything from the practice's approach, its working culture and the way its projects are photographed and presented, to the way it is exposed in the media. It is not the same as creating a brand or brand awareness.

To commission a signature building by, say, Frank Gehry is more complex than buying a Lamborghini, a Leica or a Lacoste. For architecture, the brand awareness, how it emerges and the decision-making process of acquiring 'the product' are not comparable to the world of luxury or consumer goods. 'Brands' in architecture are largely internalised and not understood by their consumers. Think of the brand awareness that would actually have to be built up if Frank Gehry or Zaha Hadid were to start a clothing line or David Adjaye a salad dressing; this would require a serious investment in marketing. From a marketing perspective, the brand potential of architecture is thus inherently low.

Identity, as opposed to brand, is about a practice having some sort of image, something that gives it a profile amongst the competition and stops it being nondescript or not worthy of media attention. Graphic designers and sisters Ellie and Katya Duffy, of Duffy Design, have worked on practice identities with a number of building-related clients, including architects. Their work has ranged from giving an identity to building sites and completed buildings through to signage that either helps communicate what is happening or directs people. Duffy Design has also designed letterheads and other pieces of graphic identity for architects. Regarding graphics and identity, Ellie Duffy says, 'Some graphic designers say it's like management consultancy. We look for the personality of the practice, what people say they are and the qualities they actually possess.' She adds, 'Coherence is what people pick up on and, to a certain level, quality'.

Is It All About Image?

**This page and opposite
Paintworks, Bristol**
Duffy Design worked with
architects Acanthus Ferguson
Mann and developers Verve
Properties to create an identity
for a converted old industrial
estate in Bristol. Graphics
worked doubly here, as a site
specific installation-like graphic
that also extends to paper,
retaining its three-dimensional
quality. In this way, the graphic
approach both helps create a
sense of place and retains it in
a logo-like treatment of the
name of the development. The
movement contained within
the graphic is also ideal for the
web

Duffy has also worked with
clients such as the Royal
Institute of British Architects
Client Services, CABE - the
Commission for Architecture
and the Built Environment,
Developer Derwent Valley and
ECD Architects. I ask, 'What is
it about architects and sans
serif fonts like Helvetica?'
Ellie says, 'In this field, there
are certain typographic norms
that stem from an education
that emphasises the modernist
tradition', to which her sister
Katya adds, 'The Bauhaus
School Machine aesthetic is
super functional and would
suggest you do not need to get
into the complexities of graphic
design by using it. Yet it is
impossible to be neutral.'

DUFFY

**This page and opposite
View, London**
The Peabody Housing Trust commissioned Duffy Design to create a platform for public consultation on its site for a mixed use development along the Grand Union Canal. The main issue was how to enable the public to see the potential of the plans. Duffy's knowledge of the construction industry was invaluable. Rather than present the public with an image that decreed what was being planned, Duffy created a viewing pavilion with etchings on glass as guidelines to what could happen on the site, allowing the public to imagine and comment on the possibilities

Is It All About Image?

It is true that for architects consistency for identity purposes is key. Say what you want to say, repeat it often enough, and rework the same few good ideas enough times and you will be persuasive. This formula has worked for quite a few architects.

Ellie Duffy explains how this clarity of approach is difficult for architects because, 'Often we work with people who are immersed in detail'. Increasingly, Duffy Design finds its role as easing the process of communication between architect and developer and vice versa, or between the project team and the general public. Ellie and Katya Duffy agree that, ultimately, graphic design is about communicating, or as Katya Duffy says, 'It is a way of thinking about things, understanding how other businesses operate, using this knowledge to help them communicate'.

Image is very much about just that, too. It effectively communicates what you want to say and reinforces it so that a picture of the practice is projected to the outside world. The term 'image' holds, perhaps, too much promise and too much negativity. Image is now implicit of trendiness, the image conscious, the vain, the shallow and the media-friendly luvvy. As a word it has gone from the pictorial to conveying an almost cynical manipulation of the truth. It is what spin doctors create in order to get the right results.

This little brochure provides a
wonderful record of a building
for a business school in
Oxford, designed by Dixon
Jones. Duffy's design suited
both the needs of the client,
the Saïd Business School
Foundation, and those of the
architects. Both parties
collaborated closely on the
project and the end result is an
accessible architectural
interpretation that does not
compromise the way the
building has been conceived.
The booklet was produced in
record time by relying heavily
on quotations from press
coverage to tell the story of the
building. This, in the absence
of a publisher, has the added
benefit of third party
accreditation for the building

The media relies on image to give a subject matter more credence than it deserves, helping it spill from the pages of newspapers onto talk shows and so on. Image sells whether it is up to scrutiny or not, it sells when building up a subject and is priceless when bringing it down. It is the stuff of the media.

Those experienced with the media understand what to expect. They a re not as often disappointed with the results as the novices in this game; instead they tend to get more out of their dealings with the media by simply understanding what it can and cannot achieve for them. As Kester Rattenbury writes in *This Is Not Architecture*, 'All media, all representations are essentially, hugely and inevitably limited, partial and biased.' She writes, 'For example, the formal elevation – perfect in time, detail and completion, with all signs of occupancy, weather, age and time edited out. The photograph – carefully framed, composed and styled, and usually empty.'

The media savvy understand what representation can achieve and the value of only telling a part of a story. They use the media as a vehicle for exposure while fully aware of its limitations. They tend to have a good rapport with the media because they do not feel cheated thanks to having realistic expectations.

My first client said three very honest things to me early on about getting a PR on board, 'You are here in part to feed our vanity, to get published, record our work the way we would like to see it'. Another day he said, 'The media exposure works for one in threes: you heard about it from someone; you read about it; the brochure arrives on your desk.' More recently he said, 'Well this is an important project to us but it's not really of interest outside the practice.' This is one of healthiest perspectives I have heard regarding why one should do PR: firstly, do it for yourself as well as a form of recognition, whether it is the best form commercially speaking or not; secondly, do it to raise interest in what you do for commercial and cultural reasons; thirdly, do it because you have a story that merits media attention.

The media have a civic purpose to voice your view of the world in public. This is quite different from doing it in private. It requires a big spirit. My conclusion is that this media game is not all about image; although it helps in getting a shot at it. At its best, the role of the media is about taking part, and about encouraging better buildings to be built through educating the public to demand them. It is about culture and the best PRS are not unlike cultural attachés.

IMAGE

JEESUS TULEE!
Image tapasi
Siperian Kristuksen

LIPPONEN GO-GO
Mikä puhemiestä riivaa?

**WARTEGGIN
SALAISUUS**
Piirrostestin tie
natsi-Saksasta
työhönottoon

Opposite
Image Lehti

The Finnish Magazine *Image* is a product of the 1980s. It coincides with a heightened interest in the cultures of advertising, design, fashion and media, and how these shape our way of thinking. The very title of the publication 'Image' has a self-irony. Are its contents about the world as portrayed through the media? On the cover here a Finnish politician is given ammunition amongst fiery graphics that are intended to portray the 'media hell' she is surviving. The story is circulated – the media writes about its own fabrications, creating what are somewhat fiction-like characters to tell better tales. Of course the promoted figure has to enter into the spirit of story telling to get covered

Below left
Content

Content, a new magazine published by Taschen and edited by Brendan McGetrick, has as its founder/editor-in-chief architect Rem Koolhaas. The publication is backed up by a PR team of six pushing the Rem Formula of 'Snapshots of the world in transition'. Features range for 'Lagos Life' to 'Prada Yada'. Koolhaas has found himself helloing the invisible cities; the result is the paper version of ether. Yet, its supporters are very real with advertising from the likes of Prada and the loyal backing of the Dutch Government

Below left
Wallpaper*

Debate about the image of design was boosted a decade later by young practices who were suffering the recession and had a lot of time to focus their energies on their media credentials as a way to get ahead. Gradually, media exposure has become very much a part of what practices expect to address when running their businesses. The likes of *Wallpaper** fed the recession generation of consumers, then in their 20s and 30s, with dreams about lifestyle. Nostalgia for the 1970s curiously worked because it played upon childhood images of glamour. The magazine was one of the first to make computer renderings of buildings a currency of the consumer media. It made styling, fashion and the surface elements of complex affairs like architecture top dollar. Together with New Labour's Cool Britannia, with its lottery-funded beauty pageants for designers, *Wallpaper** led architects to think about buildings being sexy

Bottom
This Is Not Architecture

Edited by Kester Rattenbury, published by Routledge, 2002. Definitely worth a read for a compelling insight to the workings of the architectural media. She writes that although architectural correspondents may be seen to be independent voices amongst newspaper journalists, media analysis reveals the opposite because their subject is relatively little known. Rattenbury concludes that, 'Perhaps lack of editorial subject expertise made it more essential to conform to strict news values to make sure the stories "made the papers".'

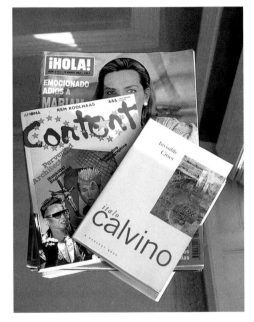

10 tips

for hiring an out-of-house PR agency

1. Does your potential agency have experience with the types of clients who understand the nuances of architectural PR? For example, do they realise the importance of the selection of the right images for a publication?

2. Does the agency know enough about the field to be able to pitch you correctly, while gauging the difference, for example, between Minimalism and High Tech, etc.?

3. Can representatives of the agency speak confidently about your projects and areas of expertise, such as sustainable design, and consider how they might be relevant to a wider audience?

4. To see how well-connected your PR is, a good test is to ring the publications you would like to be featured in and see if the editorial teams know the agency; alternatively, writers are a good source for recommending PRS

5. If you are seeking an international profile, ask at interview stage how the agency might achieve this. Consider recruiting a local PR agent overseas to work on a specific project

6. Weigh up how much press briefing you would expect an agency to do. Think about who would supply the press with the images and who has the skills to best handle these areas of PR: the agency or the practice?

7. Be wary of agencies that raise their potential clients' expectations of coverage beyond the realm of possibilities in an effort to secure a job

8. Listen out for general phrases such as 'hitting all the relevant targets'. Dig deeper to see if there is real substance there

9. Don't underestimate the time that PR takes; although cheaper than advertising, the making of a good campaign is just as labour intensive as the production of the best ads

10. Consider how dealing with your appointed out-of-house PR agency may reflect on you in the eyes of not only the press, but also your clients

10 tips for hiring an in-house publicist

1. Consider whether the person charged with PR activities is there to be reactive or proactive on behalf of the practice, and how suited their personality is for either or both

2. Too often, architects expect one person to look after desktop publishing, digital image banks, compiling information for job pitches or other publications and getting work published

3. Ask yourself whether the prospective PR should already have press contacts. Do you envision introducing the candidate to your existing contacts?

4. PR is about being switched on, punctual, thorough and polite – look for these in anyone who has a communications related title in your practice

5. In-house PRS are valuable if they stay with the practice for a long time as they develop a hard-to-replace, instant ability to find information, source the best images, and remember which clients are sensitive, etc.

6. Consider whether your in-house PR is best placed to be reactive to the needs of an out-of-house consultant by becoming their main point of contact, as well as supplying visuals and other information required

7   If the ability to write about projects is important to your PR needs, consider getting a freelance journalist to do copywriting for you or look out for an in-house PR who has published their own work

8. Don't think that academic qualifications, like a degree in art history or related subject, mean that the potential in-house PR knows a lot about contemporary architecture

9. Lots of people attracted to working in-house as PRS are creative and visually driven; they may stay longer and be happier if they work part-time whilst pursuing their own interests and projects the rest of the week

10. Be very clear about the skills required for the job from the beginning. For example, what level of desktop publishing is required? Is the in-house PR expected to know basics such as at what size to send images to publishers, or are there resources to train the person to do these small, everyday tasks efficiently?

Top 10 tips

1. Be straightforward and deliver what you promise on time

2. Don't treat people just as vehicles for your own ends but as individuals

3. Don't always talk shop at openings and meetings

4. Don't go on about your own projects but expand on topics beyond the work of your practice

5. Letters of thanks for articles written, cuttings that may interest someone and other such things go a long way to make all this more pleasant

6. Don't expect returns to be immediate; PR is always a long-term view. It's about cultivating relationships over years

7. The rules of diplomacy go a long way in PR; architects would do well to think of their promotional teams as cultural attachés who act on their behalf

8. A good contact database is worth compiling from an early stage. Too many practices draw a blank when thinking of who to invite to their 10th anniversary party or book launch

9. Be generous with books and well-presented material on the practice; too often there are far too many out-of-date copies left behind

10. Be personal, greeting people properly when they arrive, offering drinks, lunch, walking guests to the door, and offering to order a cab. Too often visitors to practices are left waiting as someone in great haste tries to find a meeting room

BIBLIOGRAPHY
GENERAL INFORMATION
PR RESOURCES

BIBLIOGRAPHY

Anon, *The Image of a Company*, Architecture Design and Technology Press (City?), 1990.

Curtis B Charles, *Multimedia Marketing for Design Firms*, John Wiley & Sons (Chichester & New York), 1996.

Wei Donget et al, *Computer Visualization, and Integrated Approach for Interior Design and Architecture*, McGraw-Hill (New York), 1998.

John E Harrigan et al, *The Executive Architect; Transforming Designers into Leaders*, (publisher?), New York, 1996.

Edgar Haupt, Manuel Kubitza, *Marketing and Communication for Architects*, Birkhäuser (Basel, Boston, Berlin), 2002.

Bart Lootsma, *SuperDutch*, Thames and Hudson (London), 2000

Veronique Patteeuw (Ed.), *City Branding, Image Building, and Building Images*, Urban Affairs Unit, Netherlands Institute for Architecture, (Rotterdam) (no year?).

Kester Rattenbury (Ed.), *This Is Not Architecture*, Routledge (London), 2002

RIBA **Marketing Department**, *An Architect's Guide to Marketing the Smaller Practice*, RIBA (London), 1989.

Brian Richardson, *Marketing for Architects and Engineers*, E&FN Spon (London), 1996.

Lynne C Ryness, *Marketing and Communication Techniques for Architects*, Longman (Harlow), 1992.

Andrew Saint, *The Image of the Architect*, Yale University (Yale), 1993.

Torsten Schmiedeknecht, *Fame*, John Wiley & Sons (Chichester & New York), 2001

Garry Stevens, *The Favored Circle*, Massachusetts Institute of Technology (Cambridge, Mass.), 1998.

Martin Symes et al, *Architects and Their Practices; A Changing Profession*, Butterworth (Oxford), 1995.

Coxe Weld et al, *Super Positioning for Architecture and Engineering Firms; Success Strategies for Design Professionals*, McGraw-Hill (New York), 1997.

Roxanne K Williamson, *American Architects and the Mechanics of Fame*, University of Texas (Austin), 1991.

GENERAL INFORMATION AND PR RESOURCES

by Laura Iloniemi and David Littlefield

PR Associations

The two main bodies in the UK that provide further information about PR consultancies are:

Institute of Public Relations

15 Northburgh Street, London EC1V 0PR
Tel +44 (0)20 7253 5151 info@ipr.org.uk www.ipr.org.uk

Public Relations Consultants' Association

Willow House, Willow Place, London SW1P 1JH
Tel +44 (0)20 7233 6026 chris@prca.org.uk www.prca.org.uk

PR MEDIA TOOLS

PR Week

Haymarket Publishing, 174 Hammersmith Road, London, W6 7JP
T +44 (0)20 8267 4429 prweek@haynet.com www.prweekuk.com

Benn's Media,

Riverbank House, Angel Lane, Tonbridge Kent, TN9 1SE
Tel +44 (0)1723 362 666 bennsmedia@ubminternational.com
www.ubminfo.com
One of the most comprehensive media listings guides, established

in 1846. It lists publications specialising in architecture and design in the UK, Europe and the rest of the world (three volumes).

PR Planner Europe/Media Disk

34 Germain Street, Chesham, Bucks, HP5 1SJ
Tel 01494 797 260 sales@pr-planner.com www.pr-planner.com
mdsales@mediainfo.co.uk www.mediadsik.co.uk
This offers a CD-ROM subscription that facilitates mailings by accessing media databases and providing targeted searches.

The Guardian Media Guide

119 Farringdon Road, London EC1R 3ER
Tel +44 (0)20 7278 2332 media.guide@guardian.co.uk
To order Tel +44 (0)870 727 4155
Media guides list useful information such details of picture agencies, picture libraries, news agencies, publishers, TV production companies and national and local newspapers. Some also have very thorough listings of both specialist and consumer magazines/periodicals. The Guardian publishes a particularly good media guide for the UK on an annual basis.

Bacon's Public Relations Guides

www.bacons.com
Much like Benn's, this is a media contacts guide with a variety of books including 'TV & Radio Only', 'NYC Only', 'Newspapers US Nationally Only". There is also an international edition as well as Bacon's On-line subscription service.

Public Relations Society of America (PRSA)

www.prsa.org
This is quite corporate, but provides newsletters, forums, lectures, panel discussions such as 'Working with celebrities' and 'How to manage high visibility litigation'.

PR Newswire

www.prnewswire.com
Established in 1954, this is a paid distribution service for sending news releases out in English, or multiple languages. It has 41 bureaus worldwide in 14 countries. Its parent company, United Business Media, is based in the UK. Journalists subscribe to its services to scout stories.

PR Newsletter

www.xpresspress.com/ipr.html
A subscription newsletter where editors and writers list the nature of stories or information they are looking for, so you can communicate directly with them. For example, a freelance travel writer might post that he/she is doing a story on the 'best island resorts' in the South Pacific. If you represent a hotel that might fit the story, you can send them information.

MARKETING ASSOCIATIONS

In terms of more mainstream marketing, the Chartered Institute of Marketing is a membership-based body which provides a comprehensive range of services including news, advice and qualifications. It also runs a Company Affiliation Programme to facilitate networking among corporate members. The CIM also runs a website.

Chartered Institute of Marketing (CIM),

Moor Hall, Cookham, Maidenhead, Berks SL6 9QH
Tel +44 (0)1628 427 500 www.cim.co.uk

MARKETING TOOLS

Marketing Week, 50 Poland Street, London, W1F 7AX
Tel ++44 (0)20 7292 3711, www.mad.co.uk
Leading magazine for the marketing trade. Its website provides a useful list of links and features; the Corporate Communications Showcase lists a wide range of PR and communications specialists.

www.marketing.co.uk
Web-based service with a comprehensive list of links and UK market data.

www.crmcommunity.co
Web-based service covering what is known as Customer Relations Management. Abundant news, research and advice is provided on the site.

ARCHITECTURAL WEBSITES

David Littlefield reviews architectural websites worth visiting:

www.ArchNewsNow.com
A great resource for anyone in the Architecture/design/urban planning field. It pulls together articles, reviews, features from newspaper around the USA and abroad and post them with links so you can actually 'scan' the daily media to keep up with criticism, and the news in the field. Free – but there is a fee to join Arc Space.

www.adam.ac.uk
The Art, Design, Architecture and Media information website has been a useful source of information across these industries, but it is due to be replaced by a new service organised by the Arts and Creative Industries (ACI) Hub. Until then, you could still try logging on to adam.ac.uk, which has a reliable and well-targeted search engine put together by professional librarians for the UK's higher education sector.

www.deathbyarch.com
Death by Architecture looks useful, with straplines including 'competitions', 'discussion' and 'resources', but it is almost impossible to get past a pop-up box congratulating you on becoming a cash-prize winner. You can access the competitions listing, though, which includes up-to-date details of architectural competitions throughout the world. Once the site gets rid of the pop-up nuisance, it promises to be a handy reference point.

www.archrecord.construction.com
The website of the Architectural Record, the authoritative USA monthly architecture title. This excellent site contains news, features and building studies, as well as useful sections covering innovation and digital practice. There is even a selection of academic essays headed 'In the cause of architecture'. Competitions are often listed in the news bulletins.

www.architecture.com/www.riba.org
Should be on the list of any architect's list of favourites. Both are run by the Royal Institute of British Architects and provide a comprehensive list of information sources, including books, images, contacts and institute policy papers. Best of all, riba.org offers the very useful Ribanet service containing a discussion forum and a 'market intelligence' section listing competitions, events and networking opportunities.

www.archguide.com
This up-to-date, English-language, Belgian site, essentially a portal for a huge array of architecture-related websites, is an invaluable resource. Clicking on any one of a long list of items (including competitions, magazines, recruitment and photography) will generate a selection of useful websites. The 'professional bodies' button generates an impressive list of national and regional architectural organisations (but strangely not the RIBA).

www.thearchitectureroom.com
Similar to archguide.com. This up-to-date site opens with details of international design competitions and contains a list of specialist subject areas which generate further lists of relevant websites – including job sites and links to CAD suppliers.

www.barbour-index.co.uk
Run by CMP, publisher of titles including Building, RIBA Journal, Building Design and Intra. The most useful aspects of the site is the wide range of technical and legal construction information that can be sourced here. The home page asked for user name and password, but you are free to browse most of the services without subscribing. Building also has its own excellent website, for which you have to register (for free). See www.building.co.uk

www.ajplus.com
Another subscription site, but this time you really do have to pay. This is a well-resourced site, with a lively discussion page. Effectively, an on-line version of the Architects' Journal.

www.archibrand.com
UK-based (but American sounding) site that has been set up to help architects and developers make the most effective use of the web. The site offers internet marketing, visualising and photographic services and will help you build your own site.

TOP FIVE INTERNATIONAL ARCHITECTURE CONFERENCES

Listed by David Littlefield:

1 MIPIM is a vast property and construction event held every spring in Cannes. Literally thousands of architects, property developers, potential clients and journalists flock to this extravaganza. See www.mipim.com

2 The International Venice Art Biennale was founded in 1893 but architecture did not get its own event until 1975. The eighth event, which took place in 2002 and was curated by Deyan Sudjic, attracted more than 100,000 visitors. See www.labiennale.org/en/architecture

3 The Alvar Aalto Symposium is an English-language international architectural conference, organised every three years in Jyväskylä, Finland. The programme aims to generate debate about the artistic, social and technical problems of modern architecture. The symposium has run eight times and is next due in 2006. Further details at www.alvaraalto.fi/conferences/symposium

4 The Royal Institute of British Architects aims to run a major architectural conference every summer. International in outlook, the event ran in Rotterdam in 2003 and used Holland as a background to explore themes concerning regeneration. Details at www.architecture.com

5 The International Union of Architects (UIA) hosts a congress every three years, bringing together thousands of architects and architecture students from around the world, providing an almost unparalleled networking opportunity. 21 events have been organised since 1948. The 2002 event took place in Berlin; the next congress is scheduled for Istanbul in 2005. See www.uia-architectes.org/count-uia.shtml

PHOTOGRAPHIC AGENCIES AND PHOTOGRAPHERS

UK AGENCIES

Arcaid
The Factory, 2 Acre Road, Kingston upon Thames, Surrey KT2 6EF
Tel +44 (0)20 8546 4352 fx +44 (0)20 8541 5230
arcaid@arcaid.co.uk www.arcaid.co.uk

arcblue.com
93 Gainsborough Road, Richmond, Surrey TW9 2ET
Tel +44 (0)20 8940 2227 fx +44 (0)20 8940 6570
arcblue@arcblue.com www.arcblue.com

Axiom Photographic Agency Ltd
The Saga Building, 326 Kensal Road, London W10 5BZ
Tel +44 (0)20 8964 9970 fx +44 (0)20 8964 8440
info@axiomphoto.co.uk www.axiomphoto.co.uk

View Pictures Ltd
14 The Dove Centre, 109 Bartholemew Road, London NW5 2BJ
Tel +44 (0)20 7284 2928 fx +44 (0)20 7284 3617
info@viewpictures.co.uk www.viewpictures.co.uk

INTERNATIONAL AGENCIES

AUSTRALIA/NEW ZEALAND

Contemporary Architecture Photography
Po Box 2505 Fortitude Valley 4006, Australia
Tel +61 2 (0)414 613 734 contact@mattkennedy.com.au
www.mattkennedy.com.au/architecture

Project Art
32 Bell Street, Seville 3139, Australia
Tel +65 (0)3 5964 2178 info@projectart.com.au
www.projectart.com.au

Paul Green Photography
3/21 Warners Avenue, Bondi Beach, NSW 2026, Australia
Tel +65 (0)4 1218 9771 pgphoto@bigpond.net

Andrew Whyte
30/2 Pohutukawa Ave, Ohope Beach 3085, New Zealand
Tel +64 (0)7 312 6222 fx +64 (0)7 312 6003
andrew@andrewwhyte.com www.andrewwhyte.com

GERMANY

Architektur Bilderservice
Am Herrenbusch 40, D-5846 Witten, Germany
Tel +49 (0)23 02 760 470 fx +49 (0)23 02 760 471
Abskandula@t-online.de www.architektur-bilderservice.de

USA

Robert Perron
Postbox 309, 119 Chestnut Street
Branford, CT 06405, USA
Tel +1 203 481 20 04 fx: +1 203 481 50 41
Office@bobperron.com www.bobperron.com

Esto Photographics Inc
222 Valley Place. Mamaroneck, NY 10543, USA
Tel +1 914 698 4060 fx 914 698 1033 esto@esto.com www.esto.com

Paul J Brokering
1320 'P' Street - Studio 300, Lincoln, NE 68508, USA
Tel +1 402 474 7744 fx 402 474 7734
paul@paulbrokering.com www.paulbrokering.com

Paul Chaplo MFA
Box T-1470, Tarleton Station, Stephenville, TX 76402, USA
info@chaplo.com www.chaplo.com

Barbara White Architectural Photography
712 Emerald Bay
Laguna Beach, CA 92651, USA
Tel +1 949 494 2479 fx +1 949 494 8227
barbara@barbarawhitephoto.com www.barbarawhitephoto.com

Red Square Photography
663 Boca Marina Court, Boca Raton. FL 33487, USA
Tel +1 561 912 9921 fx +1 561 921 9938
corey@redsquarephoto.com www.redsquarephoto.com

Cannes is renowned for its various conferences including the famous Film Festival. The property conference MIPIM takes place in the month of March. It is said to be the most lucrative of the Cannes conferences. Top dogs trot to the hills of the Mediterranean where the best parties are hosted in glitzy villas

Is It All About Image?

CONTRIBUTORS PHOTO CREDITS

ACKNOWLEDGEMENTS

Melanie Crick is based in Sydney and runs her own practice specialising in architectural communication. Her clients, from both Australia and the UK, are well-known practices that are seeking to be placed strategically in the international press. The role of PR in this process is to enhance each client's profile in particular areas where they see potential growth. This translates to a broader coverage which is not exclusive to the architectural and trade media.

Melanie's background is architectural with a mix of both practice and academic research. She is currently completing a PhD into the processes of pre-conceptual architectural thought.

Will Jones is a London-based architectural and design writer. His portfolio includes articles for *The Times* and *Financial Times*, *World Architecture*, the RIBA Journal, *Frame* and *Royal Academy Magazine*. He is also the author of two architectural books – *The Architecture of New York* and *Beyond the Brief* (available early 2005). Will's work has given him an in-depth insight into the world of architectural publicity, both good and bad. As a freelance journalist, he is very aware of how architects attempt to portray themselves and how the media sees this and reports on it. He says: 'Be straight, be informative and be yourself, then you can't get misrepresented, hopefully.'

David Littlefield is a freelance architecture writer. He has published his work in a wide variety of titles including *Blueprint*, *Frame*, *Building Design* and *Time Out*. David has also written two books – *Modern Architecture:London* and *The Architect's Guide to Running a Practice*.

David's experience of the architectural world has convinced him that good publicity can make the difference between a successful business and one that struggles. The important lesson, he believes, is that good design does not inevitably result in a higher public profile – publicity is a business tool that must be understood, planned and developed.

Ferrario Burns Hood 5, 87–9; *El Croquis* 9; Melon Studio 11–13; Nicholas Kane 15, 20–1, 116–17, 123, 125–7; Sally Tallant 16—9; Blueprint 22; Valerie Bennett 23; Arup Associates Ltd 26–7; Featherstone Associates and Caroline Wooden 28 top; Hudson Featherstone Architects 28 bottom; Photec 29 left; Fluid 29 right; Birkhäuser Verlag AG 30–1; Arup 36–7, 41–2, 97; Arup Associates Ltd/photo Caroline Sohie 38-39; Nigel Young 42, 44 bottom; Ian Lambot 43; Foster and Partners 45, 48 bottom left; www.smoothe.com, photo John MacLean 46–7, 48 top; Richard Davies (photographer)/Foster and Partners (visualisation) 48 bottom right (both); Ken Kirkwood 49; Santiago Calatrava 51; Laurence King Publishing Ltd/Santiago Calatrava photo James Brozek 52 bottom; SHoP/Sharples Holden Pasquarelli 56, 58–63; David Joseph 57; Ocean North 64–73; Alsop Architects 74–83; David Levene, 90 left; William Cross, Skycam Aerial Photography 90 right; Abitare 93; Arup/Grant Smith 95–6, 98-99; LDMC (courtesy of) 101, 103; Studio Daniel Libeskind 104, 105; Louis Hellman, first published in *World Architecture* 106; John Gollings Photography 109–11, 112 bottom; Lab + Bates Smart 112 top left and right; Trevor Mein 113; Paul Cordwell 115; Birds Portchmouth Russum 118–9, 121; David Grandorge 120; Joreon Musch 128–9; West 8 131; Laura Iloniemi (courtesy of) 140, 220; *Architectural Record* 144; Indesign Publishing 146; Merrell Publishers 147; Peter Cook/VIEW 165–73, 178; Birkin Haward, van Heyningen and Haward Architects Ltd 184–5, 186 top; Heini Schneebeli 186 bottom, 187; MGI Computer Imaging 188–9; Steven Holl 190, 192–3; RPBW 194–5; Duffy 204–5, 208; Duffy with Priestman Architects, photo Andy Keate 206–7.

A book on self-promotion is not the kind of book most architects or PRS would normally like to be seen supporting. Architects like to pretend good PR comes to them without outside specialist skills or help. They would like to believe it comes on merit alone. PRS fear their clients will mind being seen to have used consultants to promote themselves. Journalists fear that they might look as though they rely on PRS to get stories instead of discovering these themselves. Reservations are plenty. I am all the more grateful to those who assisted me in this book, for their openness and healthy sense of confidence and for their ability to give credit where credit is due.

The PR consultants who assisted me in this publication are exceptional for their intelligence, clarity of vision and honesty. Many thanks are due to Harriet Hindmarsh, Katy Harris, Peter Carzasty and Deborah Stratton. The practices I would like to thank for being particularly generous in assisting and trying to shed light how architects can better communicate with the media include: Joanna van Heyningen, Birkin Haward, Kim Holden, Kivi Sotamaa, Will Alsop, Lab Architecture, Birds Portchmouth Russum and West 8.

Of the journalists interviewed, I would particularly like to thank Robert Ivy and Robert Thiemann for their support over the years. Conversations with Edwin Heathcote, Kenneth Powell, Rory Coonan, Daniela Mecozzi and Jonathan Glancey have been invaluable. The book would not have been possible without the insights of co-authors Melanie Crick, Will Jones and David Littlefield nor the exceptional generosity of photographers Peter Cook and his picture library VIEW and Nicholas Kane who is always so accommodating and good to work with. Last but not least, developer Mel Hood has always been terrific in supporting a better understanding between the public and his work that goes beyond pure commercial interests.

INDEX

Is It All About Image?